Meetings With Angels

By the same author:

A HANDBOOK OF ANGELS

H. C. MOOLENBURGH, MD

MEETINGS WITH ANGELS

A hundred and one real-life encounters

Translated from the Dutch by
Tony Langham & Plym Peters

SAFFRON WALDEN
THE C. W. DANIEL COMPANY LIMITED

First published in Great Britain in 1992 by
The C. W. Daniel Company Limited
1 Church Path, Saffron Walden, Essex, CB10 1JP,
England

Originally published by
Uitgeverij Ankh-Hermes, Deventer, The Netherlands
with the title *Een engel op je pad*

ISBN 0 85207 260 0

Reprinted 1993

Designed by Tina Ranft
Production in association with
Book Production Consultants Plc, Cambridge

Typeset by Rowland Phototypesetting Ltd
Bury St Edmunds, Suffolk
Printed and bound by
St Edmundsbury Press Ltd
Bury St Edmunds, Suffolk

CONTENTS

For my dear An

A Word Of Thanks

In the first place, I would like to warmly thank all those people who wrote to me spontaneously about their experiences with angels, and later gave me their permission to publish their stories so that I could write this book. Unfortunately, there were one or two people I was unable to contact, as well as some people who have died. I would like to thank those who were unable to answer my letters for any reason, and the relatives of those who have died, and assure them that their experiences with angels will not be lost.

I would also like to thank all those people who sent me excerpts from books and magazines which I have used in this book. They made an important contribution.

I am pleased to thank the publishers of books and magazines who gave me permission to quote them. They are mentioned in the bibliography.

In addition, I would like to thank my publishers, Paul Kluwer and Nicole de Haas, who gave me so much encouragement to write this book. And last, but by no means least, my warm gratitude goes to Emilie Schreuder. She painstakingly corrected this manuscript, not only removing many spelling mistakes and above all stylistic errors, but also contributing extremely valuable ideas about improving the composition and enriching the contents.

She was able to do this partly because of the wisdom passed on to her by her father, the former headmaster of the Montessori Lyceum in Amsterdam, a dear friend of mine who died recently. His lessons on style and content live on in this book, and I would gratefully like to remember him here.

FOREWORD

I t is a daunting prospect to write a second book about
the same subject, especially when the first book was a
success. One is inclined to think that the success of the
first book has gone to the author's head.
Therefore I waited a number of years before starting on
it, despite requests from many people to write more
about angels. The reason I went ahead anyway is this.
Since the publication of *Angels as the Protectors and Helpers
of Man* at Christmas, 1983, there has been a constant
stream of 'angel mail' which I am still receiving now.
More than five hundred people have written to me. Three
hundred and fifty of these letters came from the Netherlands; the rest from abroad. The book was also published
in German and English*, and I actually received letters
from Argentina, Austria, Belgium, Canada, Curaçao,
England, Finland, France, Germany, Israel, Italy, Poland,
Scotland, Sweden, Switzerland and the United States.
In addition, people have sent me books, drawings,
poems, cassettes, embroidered angels, straw angels, stone
angels, and magazines, i.e., such a varied range of articles
relating the angels that I felt quite overwhelmed. I was

* Published under the title *A Handbook of Angels* by The C. W.
Daniel Company.

also extremely moved by the warmth and friendship of all these generous people.

The stream of letters and gifts was further encouraged because the press paid a great deal of attention to the 'doctor who was seeing things' – as one newspaper put it – and because I was also asked to give interviews for magazines, and on radio and t.v. In 1989, I was even asked to give my views on angels for the B.B.C. in England during the Christmas period. It seemed that I was suddenly considered to be a sort of expert on angels, undoubtedly to the great amusement of the angels themselves.

Fortunately, I constantly had my leg pulled by one of my sons, who made disparaging remarks like: 'We'll soon have "Return of the Angels" and "The Angels Strike Back".' He'll undoubtedly be quite tickled, now that Part Two is really being published.

The letters included no less than one hundred and forty from people who had themselves had authentic experiences with angels, some even several times in their lives. These are really the true angel experts. Altogether there were over one hundred and fifty angel experiences amongst the more than five hundred letters. Many of these were so special and so instructive that I did not believe it was right to keep my collection to myself.

This then is the reason that I decided to write a second book after all. By no means all of the wonderful experiences have been included in this book. This is not because I wish to keep anything back for Part Three, but because many experiences are variations on a particular theme. Therefore I tried as far as possible to give examples of different themes.

Several times in the past few years I have tried to put together all this material in a readable form, but without success. However, in February 1991, I was asked to give my views about an angel event in the programme 'Tijdsein' ('Sign of the Times'). During that interview I realized how I could write the book. Up to then I had tried to let the people who had written the letters speak for themselves about their moving experiences, but this produced an untidy and chaotic result. It is quite a different thing to read a letter in the handwriting of the person who wrote it from reading the same letter printed in a book.

A great deal of the atmosphere is lost, and I could not find a way of reproducing it properly. However, during the programme I suddenly saw a way of writing the new book so that it would hang together as a whole, by retelling in my own words the stories contained in the letters. This means you are actually working like a painter, who is admittedly reproducing a true likeness in a portrait, but in addition reveals something about his own relationship to his subject, so that the painting is more than just a photograph.

Once I understood that I could process the letters just like a painter works on his canvas, the book wrote itself.

To what can I compare the work that is in front of you? At the beginning of 1991, there was a beautiful exhibition in the Nieuwe Kerk in Amsterdam of the art treasures from the San Marco in Venice. Most of these treasures had originally been plundered from Constantinople by the Venetians. They included goblets entirely encrusted with gems, with feet set with small enamel paintings. Each medallion represented a Christian saint. All these serious ascetic faces stared out of the foot of the goblet, and it was a mystery how the artist had been able to paint this on the enamel.

I would like to use one of these goblets as a symbol for this book: small, precise paintings of deeply religious experiences. The content of this 'goblet' was given to me in many letters. Occasionally the content is rather difficult, and it is best to enjoy it in small sips, so that you do not have too much at any one time.

Of course, I asked the permission of the people whose stories I used, to publish them. However, they are very personal matters, and therefore I feel rather like the Venetian merchant who plundered Constantinople. In writing this book, I have become a sort of Merchant of Venice. Therefore I will end this foreword with a reflection taken from Shakespeare's *Merchant of Venice*. In the last scene of this comedy Lorenzo observes the heavens. He calls it 'the floor of the heaven'. 'There's not the smallest orb which thou beholdest / But in his motion like an angel sings'. Lorenzo summons up mighty choirs of angels in our imagination, who sing for the delight of the eternally youthful cherubim. He conjures up a shining golden heaven, full of heavenly music, following in the footsteps of the *Book of Job*. In chapter 38, the Lord answers Job from a storm. Speaking about the earth, he asks Job: 'Whereupon are the foundations thereof fastened, or who laid the cornerstone thereof, when the morning stars sung together, and all the sons of God shouted for joy?'

Lorenzo concludes his thoughts by saying 'Such harmony is there in immortal souls.'

In a time when people seem to think that there is nothing more important than the stock market quotations or the latest television programmes, it is good to be reminded what life on earth is really about: the awakening of the immortal soul and its joyful singing in the harmony of the spheres.

N.B. To protect their privacy, I have made sure that the people who had these experiences with angels cannot be identified from their stories. However, I have been in personal contact with all of them. I know their names, and the exact places where the experiences occurred.

In the few cases where I do not, I have made a special note.

CHAPTER 1

AN ANGEL BY THE ROADSIDE

In January 1991, a strange story was told. A Dutchman, driving his car along the motorway, picked up a hitchhiker. When the car was once again travelling at considerable speed, the hitchhiker suddenly started to warn the driver in a serious tone that Jesus was on the point of returning. The driver looked round at him rather pityingly, and realized, to his intense shock, that he was in the car alone. The hitchhiker seemed to have vanished into thin air. Badly frightened, he parked his car on the hard shoulder, where a traffic policeman soon stopped to ask him what he was doing there. The policeman then helped the man, who was in a fairly distraught condition. The so-called 'Angel on the motorway' was a great success in evangelical circles. There was a great deal of speculation about it from every quarter. A vicar spoke on the subject from the pulpit, articles appeared in magazines, and even radio and t.v. devoted some time to it. A sergeant from the traffic police inserted a message in the police newspaper, asking the policeman concerned to come forward. The strange thing is that this story was not new. Although it was described as having 'just happened', the story was much older. In 1983, a similar rumour was circulating in Germany. There, it went as follows:

A driver saw a hitchhiker standing by the motorway, a

young man wearing an anorak and jeans, and carrying a rucksack on his back. Once in the car, the young man said he was the Angel Gabriel, and that he was coming to announce the end of the world. Then this 'angel' also vanished from the moving car without trace. The story was even published in a regional newspaper, and confirmed to me by two independent sources in January and April 1984.

Differences between the two stories are very slight. In Germany, the hitchhiker's clothes were described, he called himself 'Gabriel' and predicted the end of the world.

In the Netherlands, he did not say he was an angel, let alone Gabriel. His clothes were not described, and he announced not the end of the world, but the return of Jesus. Curiously, the police were involved, and a burly police sergeant even appeared on television, to have his say.

Both versions refer to hitchhiking on the motorway (i.e., a traffic offence), a prediction, and a sudden disappearance.

The stories have one other thing in common: they cannot be verified. Everyone who tells the story has heard it second hand. No one knows anyone who was directly involved. This means that the whole affair can be categorized as what is known in my part of the Netherlands as a 'monkey roll' story. In case the reader is not familiar with this sort of story, here is an example. My aunt has a cleaning lady whose niece told her that in Amsterdam there's a butcher who sells rolls with monkey's meat. It must be true, because the other day I heard it from a man whose brother's wife had been told so herself by the baker, whose eldest son had eaten a monkey roll.

Everyone believes the monkey roll story, but no one knows exactly who was involved, or where it took place. I came across the first example of the 'Angel on the motorway' story in Ethel Portnoy's book, *Monkey Roll*, which she published in 1979. Not only had she heard the story at about that time, but she had also read it in the magazine *Panorama* (15 July 1977). She noted that it was a modern version of a story which was already being told in the Middle Ages.

All this means that it is improbable that the 1991 version of the motorway angel is a brand-new true story. But it is worth analyzing the background in more detail. The first question which arises is this: was there an angel who hitchhiked on the motorway, either in the Netherlands in 1991, or in Germany in 1983? The best we can do is to try and answer this question with the help of Occam's razor. The philosopher, William of Occam (eleventh century), laid down the rule that when you are looking for the solution to a problem, the most obvious explanation is usually the correct one. In other words: If five-year-old Johnny is standing in the kitchen looking naughty, and the biscuit tin turns out to be empty, the chance that he has scoffed all the biscuits is much greater than the chance that Johnny's own story is true, viz, that a strange man walked into the kitchen, put his hand in the biscuit tin, and quickly ran away. Even if Johnny insists that his story is true, the real explanation of the missing biscuits – according to Occam's razor – is still that Johnny has eaten them.

If we apply Occam's razor to the angel on the motorway, there are two options:

1. The Angel Gabriel, or at least *an* angel, was hitching along the motorway and frightened the life out of a driver.

2. It is a 'monkey roll' story, produced by the rich imagination of the human mind, which fell on sufficiently fertile ground to allow the story to grow.

According to Occam's razor, version 2 is correct.

Just analyze this case. Why would an angel predict the end of the world or the return of Jesus? (After making a driver commit a traffic offence.) Why would the angel choose someone who does not know what to make of the story and is frightened almost senseless?

Gabriel is not unknown to us. We know something about his character. He explained the vision of the ram and the kid to the prophet Daniel (Daniel 8), he told Daniel about the coming of the Messiah (Daniel 9), he predicted the coming of John the Baptist to Zachariah the Priest, and announced the birth of Jesus to Mary shortly afterwards (Luke 1).

Every time, Gabriel acted in such a way and in such a place that his message had the maximum effect.

In contrast, the angel on the motorway merely gave rise to a rather sensational shock, and the effect of his spectacular disappearance only caused great alarm.

The messages of angels are also characterized by great accuracy: 'And behold, thou shalt conceive in thy womb, and shalt bring forth a son', (Luke 1:31) or: 'Thou shalt be dumb . . . because thou believest not my words' (Luke 1:20), or: 'For unto you is born this day a saviour . . .' (Luke 2:11). On the other hand, the message of the angel on the motorway is vague. The end of the world? What does he mean? It is as though the motorway angel has connections with the *Watchtower* community. The return of Jesus? Didn't Jesus himself say that he would return 'like a thief in the night', and that nobody knew 'at what hour the thief would come'? (Matthew 24:36 and 43) However, suppose that we are concerned here with a rumour, a story which circulates for an unknown reason, as many rumours do. This explanation is much more likely, and I think that with regard to stories about angels, we should always retain a healthy skepticism. If we do this, the true stories will emerge all the more clearly. Thus, to sum up, this is not an angel story, but a 'monkey roll' story. Then you may wonder where the rumour came from in the first place.

I cannot say much about the rumour which circulated in 1983, but obviously the months of January and February 1991 were charged with predictions of doom. The aerial bombardment of the Iraqi dictator, Saddam Hussein, started on 15 January, and the ground war, which was to have such disastrous consequences for the environment, on 24 February, although it was all over surprisingly quickly.

In Arabic, Saddam's name means 'I confront', but in Hebrew, it is the same name as Sodom, which means 'a destructive sea of fire'. When we remember the photographs of the burning oil wells in Kuwait, he certainly seems to live up to his name.

This man, who rebuilt the ancient city of Babel, cannot but speak to the imagination of Christians, Jews and Muslims. He succeeded in unleashing primitive memories in the unconscious layers of the human spirit. For a while it was as though the ancient Babylonian kingdom between the two rivers had come back to life, and against this background, a rumour like that of an angel by the motorway, easily takes wing. Just at the place where we are roaring along the motorways in petrol-powered cars, a traveller suddenly appears predicting the end of the world. We were overwhelmed with t.v. images of billions of litres of oil uselessly flowing into the Persian Gulf, and of billions of litres more going up in greasy black smoke, and there was a disquieting sense that perhaps there would be no more oil. Would life, as we knew it, be over? During the Gulf War many people had such feelings that the end of the world was at hand, and – suddenly, there was the angel, announcing the end of the world, or at least, the coming of Jesus, who is often associated with the end of the world as we know it.

Therefore I see the 'angel by the motorway' more as a psychological projection of a sense of impending doom in the world than as the visit of a celestial messenger.

Let us not forget that at the end of the first millenium, people also had a sense that the world was coming to an end. We are now nearing the end of the second millenium after Christ, and have even more reason than ever for feeling that the end of the world is nigh.

Perhaps many people will be disappointed by this view. In this day and age – which can be very hard – there is a great need for consolation and help from mysterious other worlds. People can take it amiss when you shatter their illusions. And yet, it is important to do this, for otherwise we would not be able to assess the value of true angel stories. In the rest of this book we are concerned with true angel stories, and I will begin with the question: does this mean there are no angels along our motorways?

Of course there are, just listen.

1   It was a beautiful sunny day in May 1982 in Limburg. A nice young couple with a daughter aged one and a half parked their car by a cheerful café at the side of a busy motorway and sat down on the terrace. The sun was shining and they felt relaxed. A waiter took their order, and little Anna pottered around. In front of the café the traffic roared past relentlessly.

In this relaxed atmosphere, it is all too easy to forget to

be on your guard for just a moment. Suddenly the parents wondered in a panic where Anna had got to. They looked around, and to their horror noticed that the toddler had managed to climb down the terrace and was now wandering straight towards the extremely busy motorway. It was too late to stop her. Nevertheless, the parents jumped up in a panic, the father chasing after the child, the mother just behind him. Then suddenly, just before Anna was about to walk into the road, a lovely, sweet little blond girl about four years old, walked up. She stood between the toddler and the road, spread out her arms, and stopped Anna. A moment later the ashen-faced father reached his daughter, picked her up and said: 'Never walk away from Mummy and Daddy again.' The mother also arrived, and they bent over to thank the little girl who had saved their child. There was no little girl to be seen. The road was in front of them. The stairs to the terrace behind them, the car-park and pavement to the left and right. It was impossible that the child could disappear, but she had vanished into thin air.

This true miracle occurred in Limburg (1982) in a very modest, quiet way, a year before the stories about the Angel Gabriel on the motorway in Germany (1983).

A fake angel hitchhiking by the road; a true angel modestly carrying out her work of salvation.

How touching it was that this guardian angel assumed the form of a little girl. A toddler might have stepped back in panic if it had been a big man, and might still have been crushed by a car, but a sweet little girl is just fun and interesting to a toddler. When God appears in the form of his servants, he is often characterized by modesty. It is not surprising that in this age of mass mobility, meetings with angels and cars often go together.

Here is another story which took place in the Pyrenees in 1982.

2 On the day that this story starts, the conditions in the mountains were bitter. A gale force storm was raging, and it was snowing so hard that the roads were soon impassable. A middle-aged married couple were driving

straight through this storm on the road from Prades to
Bourg-Madame at a height of 1500 m. The road was
narrow and twisting. Later, they found out that this was
the worst storm that there had been for sixty years. Just
imagine the conditions: the driving snow, a steep rock
wall to the left, a deep ravine on the right. The wheels
of the car would no longer grip the increasingly slippery
road surface, and gusts of wind blowing at 140 kilometres
per hour shook the car. The driver decided to put the
snow chains on the wheels, and drove the car to a spot
where there was a recess in the rock wall. Unfortunately
the manoeuvre failed, and the car ended up straight across
the road. When he tried to move, the car slipped and
stopped at the edge of the ravine. The situation was truly
life-threatening. Visibility was extremely poor, and the
chance that someone coming the other way would crash
into them – so that they would all plunge into the ravine
– was by no means unlikely. The driver made one more
attempt to pull away, but this time the car really almost
slid into the ravine. Although it was bitterly cold, the
sweat broke out on the driver's brow. What should he
do? There wasn't a house anywhere nearby from which
he could fetch help. He realized that he had never in his
life put on snow chains, though he did have them with
him. Would he manage in the middle of a blinding snow-
storm, right on the edge of a ravine? Then, quite unexpectedly, as though he had fallen from heaven, a man walked
up. He looked about forty years old, was simply and
neatly dressed, and had a friendly face. He did not say
anything, but pushed the car away from the ravine without any difficulty, into the recess in the rock wall on the
other side of the road. Then, still without saying a word,
he took the snow chains out of the boot, fitted them onto
the wheels in a jiffy, and started to walk away. The driver
couldn't thank him enough, and wanted to give the man
some payment, but he refused it, smiling. 'Give the
money to someone else', said the driver, and pressed a
banknote into the man's hand anyway. The man said
goodbye, turned round, walked off in the opposite direction from which he had come, and suddenly vanished
without trace.
So he obviously had not come from a car parked a little
further on, or he would have walked back in the direction

from which he had come. It was only then that the couple became aware of the strangest thing of all. The man had come walking through the snow storm, had fitted the snow chains, and had gone again. They had seen all this quite clearly, and yet the man had not had a snowflake on him. It was as though the snow had not existed for him.

The couple took another good look at the recess in the rock face. It was a sort of drive, leading to a small cave, rather like the cave in Lourdes.

With the help of the snow chains, they finally succeeded in reaching a little village two hours later, after a very difficult drive. These people live in Andorra, and they often drive along that road. They told me that every time they pass the little lane to the cave, they feel a sense of jubilation.

So was that really an angel by the roadside?

Yes, it probably was. The couple were certainly in danger of their lives. Later the military went into the mountains to have a good look for stranded drivers. Even if they had not driven into the ravine, they could easily have frozen to death. The unknown 'man' appeared from nowhere, a long way from the civilized world, resolved an almost hopeless situation in a few minutes, and then vanished back into nothingness. It seemed – and this is very important – as though the snow could not touch him. It was as though he lived partly in another world where it was not snowing. He left behind him a clear and long-lasting feeling of joy.

In addition, there is the curious fact that the couple only really became aware that the snow did not settle on him, after he had gone. Contact with heaven often produces a dream-like change of consciousness, so that something which might have seemed bizarre or strange at another time, now seems normal, or goes unnoticed. In our dreams we do not think it is strange that we can fly, although we know that this is impossible when we are awake. Thus in this situation, there was clear evidence of a slight change in consciousness.

All the things I have mentioned here are classic character-istics of true meetings with angels. The whole story con-trasts sharply with the 'Angel by the motorway'. That story had a rather ghostly and sinister quality, while the story in the Pyrenees was heartwarming and almost radiated light. The world in which we live is much stranger than we think, and the boundaries between this world and other worlds are not hermetically sealed: there are gaps which occasionally become visible.

The following rather bizarre story is an example of these strange gaps in the dividing wall to another world. If it were not for the fact that I have known the woman involved in these events for thirty-three years, and know that she is very reliable and has no tendency to hallucinate or imagine things, I wouldn't have dared to include this story in my book. It is not quite a story about angels, although what I am about the describe could not have happened without angels.

3 When these events occurred, the woman was 50 years old. She was driving her car along a main road, travelling towards a crossroads at considerable speed. It was the middle of the day, there was no fog, and visibility was good.

Just at the moment that she was crossing over the crossroads – where she had priority – a large lorry came hurtling towards her from the left, straight over the crossroads. There was absolutely no possibility of avoiding it, for the lorry was driving straight towards the side of her car. But in a flash, something unbelievable happened. The lorry became transparent, and drove through her car without a sound. Then it reappeared on the other side of her car, as solid as ever, and simply drove on. You could almost describe this as a case of dematerialization and materialization. But these are only words to try and explain the inexplicable.

It all seems too strange to be true. The woman immediately told her children what had happened to her, and everyone agreed that it was a miracle.

Yet this story is not unique.

When my book, *Angels*, had been on the market for a few months, I was phoned by a friendly-sounding woman who asked me whether I would like to come and talk about it on a live t.v. show. This was a programme with Sonja Barend (the well-known Dutch chat show hostess).

Let me first explain that for many years I was opposed to owning a television set. At first, I didn't want one because the programmes seemed unsuitable for my children in their growing years – of course, they secretly watched television elsewhere – and later, because it seemed to be a waste of time. Perhaps you can guess what happened next. For my sixtieth birthday my dear children gave me a splendid colour t.v., and since then, to their unconcealed delight, I have enjoyed watching t.v. very much. However, this was the reason that in 1984 I had no idea who Sonja Barend was. I told the woman that I would come, and the next day I phoned my second son, who was fairly familiar with t.v. programmes. 'Have you ever heard of Sonja Barend?' I asked him in all innocence. He couldn't stop laughing, and then said: 'Dad, don't tell me that you're going to be on her show.' Of course, I had to tell him that I was, and asked him why this was so funny. 'Oh', he said, 'you often see people have a go at each other in those shows. She likes to organize cockfights. I don't think you've ever done anything as crazy as that. I'm going to come and watch.' A few weeks later, I was sitting round the table with Sonja. In the meantime, I'd heard a great deal about her, how sharp she was, how incisive, how you had to be on your guard. But when I was sitting next to her, I didn't notice any of these things. I immediately liked her.

What you see on t.v. is completely different from what you see in reality. The t.v. is brilliant at giving a false impression of people. Sonja had brought together a number of people who had had strange experiences, and asked me to comment on them.

4 One of these people was a man who told me how, as he was driving along a dual carriageway in thick mist, he was overtaking a car when he suddenly saw headlights coming straight towards him out of the mist. A head-on collision was unavoidable, and in his case the impossible happened as well: the car driving towards him became hazy, and silently passed through his car. A moment later, he saw the red rear lights disappearing in his rear-view mirror. He had miraculously escaped certain death.

5 A third story from my collection concerns a man driving a moped almost alongside a lorry. At a side road the lorry suddenly turned right, and the man on the moped went at full speed into the side of the lorry. At least, he thought he did. But a moment later he noticed that he was riding on in the direction he had been going, and he saw to his utter amazement that the lorry was travelling along the side road as though nothing had happened. The only evidence of a 'collision' was the pannier on the back of his moped, which had been thrown a long way through the air. What seemed physically impossible – two solid objects taking up the same space – had actually happened! The moped had gone straight through the lorry.

Thus we must assume that we are concerned here with another dimension, which suddenly produces space where there could normally not be any. Just think of the famous example of two-dimensional creatures living in a flat plane, for whom the third dimension represents a miraculous world. Suppose that the character Piet, whom I am writing about here, is alive and looking at you. On either side of him are his two friends 'character' and 'which', though – as he cannot look around the corner, he can only see the letter 'r' on his right, and 'w' on his left. Now just imagine that Piet can suddenly jump up from this page. In his world this is not possible, because it is two-dimensional. He would suddenly disappear from the world of 'character' and 'which', and even if he returned, he could go back before the word 'character' or after the word 'which'. This would be a miracle for 'character' and 'which'. This is more or less how I imagine that the people in the stories recounted above were saved through the fourth dimension.
In fact, these stories are actually like stories about angels in reverse.
Experiences with angels often involve a threatening situation which is suddenly resolved by a figure appearing from nowhere. In the near collision cases, the car which is hurtling forwards disappears into nothingness just before the shattering impact, and then reappears when the danger spot has been passed. In the angel stories, the angel becomes visible for a moment and then disappears,

while in these stories the car becomes invisible for a moment, and then reappears.

So why are there so many fatal head-on collisions? Why do so many toddlers walk out and get hit by cars? Why is it that some drivers do plunge into ravines?

I suspect that in this three-dimensional world, disaster is the normal course of events. This is a world in which accidents lurk round every corner, as viewers of *Rescue 911* will confirm. This programme reveals a constantly recurring pattern. It always begins more or less idyllically with a young couple on holiday, or a family in a nice little house, or a young girl in her room on her own, reading a book. And you know what's going to happen. A sudden crash on the road, a burst of flame, a burglar intent on rape, and you're on the edge of your chair. Disaster and disease are part of our world. They are normal. The extraordinary thing is that there are exceptions. There are holes in the web of Creation. Usually we do not see them, we pass them by, but under special conditions, the hole suddenly becomes visible. Then it appears that there is a window or a door to another world.

Is there something special about the people who have had such an extraordinary experience, or is it coincidence?

It is difficult to say anything about this. The people who have had these experiences are people like you and I, though with the difference that something about them does change after such an experience. They can never be quite the same again, for their locked world has become an open world, and they have realized that there are openings in the 'watertight' system.

I can only voice my suspicion that those who have these experiences were in some way ready for them. They had arrived at a point in their lives where they were given just the shock to change their lives.

The principle is reminiscent of aspects of Zen Buddhism. A pupil of Zen is given a riddle by his master. The riddle consists of a particular sentence, which cannot be solved logically, such as: 'What is the sound of one hand clapping?' The pupil will meditate for months on this riddle without arriving at an answer. Finally, he appears before his master, who unexpectedly gives him a hard blow, and suddenly his whole psychic structure is transformed.

He is now 'enlightened'. The cards of his being have been reshuffled, he has become a different person, and sees the world from a completely different perspective. There is no external change, the change is an inner change.

In the same way, I believe that those people who unexpectedly have an experience with angels, may have been brought to that point in their lives where meditation took the Zen pupil. There is a sort of critical current, and then one single directed blow – and the person is changed for ever. Therefore I suspect that the person who had the experience with angels was quite 'ready' for it at that precise moment.

Nature all around us also reveals these sporadic transitions. First, there is a straggly little green plant, and the next day it is transformed into a bright yellow flowering crocus. There is a nest of eggs, and then suddenly there are four little naked blackbirds craning their necks.

One of the skills in life is to recognize these crossroads or sudden transitions. If you fail to recognize them, you inadvertently stray off the path. The Zen master's blow with a stick is needed at this moment of transition.

Ouspensky and Nicoll say that the life of a person, or the life of a group of people, passes according to the laws of the tonic solfa.

First, there is the beginning, the birth of a person, a club, an idea. That is the base note, the doh.

Then there is the path which proceeds from here: the child growing up, the development of the new club, the spreading of the idea. That is the second note, the re.

This is followed by consolidation; the person gets some grip on life (the stage of the school-age child), the club becomes organized, the idea acquires a set structure.

Everyone knows what this sounds like: do, re, me. There is an interval between the do and the re, the same interval between the ray and the me, a regular progression.

But the next tone is the fa, and the interval between the me and the fa is smaller, a minor second. It is a sort of transitional point, a problem area.

This may be rather difficult to understand, and therefore I would like to explain it in more detail. Ouspensky's system is based on the following idea: creation flows down from above, and this occurs in particular waves of

energy. These energies are arranged like a descending
scale: do–si–la–sol–fa–me–re–do.

Imagine this energy like a stream. Whenever there is a
whole interval between two notes, the stream is flowing
regularly. Where the interval is a semitone, the stream
narrows. The water is suddenly flowing harder, and
seethes. In our development, we, as people, move the
other way. We start at do, and then slowly work our
way up to the next do. Therefore all true development
is against the current. The extra difficult points are the
places where the stream flows more quickly. If you want
to swim against the current, you need extra energy.
These are the moments at which a person or a group of
people become stuck.

In man, this is reflected in puberty; in a society it is seen
in the rigidity imposed by an autocratic chairman; the
idea has finally come up against exceptions and does not
work as well as it originally seemed to. At this point,
extra attention and extra energy are needed. The adolescent struggles with himself and with his parents; society
is unbalanced by angry members or an idea is adapted or
rejected. Sometimes things can go wrong. The opportunity provided by the transition point is missed, and the
path is deflected. An adolescent may become hooked on
drugs, a society may become stultified, an idea can
become dogma. Everyone is familiar with examples of
this sort of thing. The idealistic organization which
spends more and more money on dinners for the board
of directors. The doctor who begins as an idealist with
the burning desire to help his fellow man, but treats more
and more people, giving them less and less time because
he has to pay for his practice. The liberation of the
oppressed worker which ends up with the whole working
population being enslaved.
I get the impression that experiences with angels take
place when the stream of life narrows in this way. The
person involved is not usually conscious of the fact that
he is at a transitional point, the moment when me changes
to fah. And yet, this is the interval at which this stream
of life narrows, just like a river becomes narrower when
it passes through a mountain chasm. The water flows

faster, and in life there is a similar speeding up of the current. In this situation, the angel appears like an unexpected smile from heaven. Then the stream of life broadens out again, and everything is changed.

The next note is the sol, and it is not for nothing that this comes from the word meaning 'sun'. There is a glow which can never again fade away completely. For the person involved and those around him, this is a sign that the path is not without a goal. There is a structure in the path, just as there is a structure in the process of a plant growing and flowering. Admittedly we have been sown here on earth, but our goal is elsewhere. Potentially there is a new person concealed within everyone, and our whole life – whether we like it or not – is aimed at allowing that new person to be born. Man here on earth is a larva, a caterpillar, and his goal is to be transformed into a dragonfly or butterfly. The meeting with angels is not meant only to help someone out of their difficulties; this experience serves a greater purpose, and is particularly intended to help man in his metamorphosis from caterpillar to butterfly.

Angels are not an ambulance crew from heaven, who spring into action to help drivers in distress. They are more like doctors delivering babies, who help to bring about the rebirth of man.

Jesus said: 'Except a man be born again, he cannot see the kingdom of God' (John 3:3).

This text does not refer to reincarnation, as some people seem to think. It is about inner rebirth, about the new man who is born from the old larva.

If a meeting with an angel does not contribute to the inner rebirth of the person involved, it has no meaning. That is why the ghostly angel on the motorway was meaningless. But the angel who saved the toddler was an initial impulse to give form to the magnificent butterflies which will at some point be born from that toddler's parents and from the little girl herself.

By now, the reader may be under the impression that all angels have something to do with cars.

Obviously this is not the case. It only means that the setting does do not have to be in the countryside or paradisaical for them to appear. Come with me to a place as prosaic as a railway station with an escalator leading down to the platforms.

6 In 1984, an elderly couple was travelling by train. They got off in Utrecht and took the escalator leading to the platform. First, the man stepped onto the escalator, and the woman followed. Then she had one of those typical unfortunate accidents that can happen anywhere. The heel of her shoe was trapped in something, and she fell back. At the same moment, she felt two powerful hands holding her arms, and heard a voice which said: 'Keep going, keep going.' Her husband, who happened to look round, saw a big man standing just behind her, supporting her. When they got to the top of the escalator, she turned round to thank the man who had helped her. There was no one to be seen. Her husband could not see him either.

I like this sort of story, because there are two witnesses. Something of the rebirth which takes place in a woman who experiences this sort of thing is reflected in the following poem. It was included in the same letter which described the incident on the escalator.

> Eternity moves my heart
> And bears me through time.
> Over the boundaries into the sphere
> Of Your glory.
>
> I wander like Henoch
> So close by Your side,
> And as a consolation rustling through my soul,
> Suffering has passed.
>
> And eternal youth is on my head.
> Yes, I am a king's child,
> And will find the path leading upwards,
> Together with Him.

This little poem expresses what I mean more clearly than any words can: we see a person moving from a closed to an open world.

When we are told about heaven, we look up inadvertently, although the heaven of the angels obviously is not situated perpendicularly above the ground below. Moreover, it seems right and meaningful when angels appear in high mountains. You might almost say that they belong there, more than along the motorway.

7 The following story is set in the Dolomites. The woman who told it to me was walking with her husband, 3000 m up in the mountains. They had climbed up and had lunch in a hut. At three o'clock they started to return. Up to then it had been a radiant day, but suddenly the sun disappeared and the sky turned dark grey. Before they knew what was happening, they were walking along an icy path which led along the edge of a deep abyss. At first they were not aware of the danger they were in, but at a certain point the path became really slippery, and to make matters even worse, her husband, who was walking in front of her, suffered an attack of vertigo. In that sort of situation, you don't know what to do. Is it best to stand still? But what happens then? Should you go on? But suppose you plunge down into the abyss.

At one point the path disappeared entirely, and an enormous sheet of ice stretched in front of them. They would have to cross it to get to the cable car which would take them back to the valley. She gave her husband a hand, and they carefully set foot on the sheet of ice, keeping their eyes straight ahead because of the abyss, which seemed to have a magnetic force. She was very frightened, and prayed softly: 'Please help us, God.' At that moment she heard steps cracking the ice behind her. Feeling very irritated, she thought this was the last straw, being chased from behind, on top of everything else. So she called out in German to the person behind them, not to take any notice of them, but to pass them by.

Then she heard a soft, penetrating voice behind her. She heard the German words: 'I just want to help you.' The voice radiated love and peace, and she immediately said, 'Oh please, please help me.'

She felt two hands holding her arms from behind, and in a moment they had crossed the dangerous sheet of ice. It seemed to have taken only a few seconds. The hands let her go, and from the bottom of her heart she said,

'Thank you'. Then she looked round, but there was no one there, only the total emptiness of the lonely mountain landscape. The strange thing is that she finished the story by asking, 'Was that really an angel?' You will notice that they spoke German, although this couple came from the Netherlands. I believe that this is another example of the phenomenon we encountered before. Angels do not wish to frighten anyone. For a small child, an angel can appear as a child; for this woman, who expected the person behind her to speak German, he was a German-speaking hiker. It was actually important that she was not frightened in any way, for a sudden movement at that point could have been fatal for the couple. Perhaps I should put it a different way. An inhabitant of heaven speaks in our head and we hear the language we expect. What ever the case may be, the couple were saved. I know her well; she still has a look of surprise in her eyes.

8 This is another similar story which took place in the mountains. The wife of an American writer was corresponding with a ninety-year-old lady in southern Germany. She was writing about my first book on angels – which is obviously very flattering for an author. The American woman wrote that she believed in guardian angels and had a reason for this. She lived in the Ozarks, a rather rough mountainous area in Arkansas. She had made a footpath along a canyon which was not too deep, and where she liked to go on solitary walks. One day, as she was making one of these walks, she had to jump over a stream running straight across the road, which plunged into the canyon next to her. She had done this countless times, and so she jumped from a rock to the other side, but this time she slipped, turning and twisting like a spinning top. She lost her balance and fell down. In a flash, she saw what would happen: she would fall onto the rocks in a deeper part of the canyon, and would be killed, or at least seriously injured.

No sooner had she realized this, than she felt that she was floating through the air like the airborne fluff of a dandelion clock. She floated on the air, just as you can float on water. As lightly as a feather, she was put down on the rock from which she had jumped. It was an indescribable force which had carried her. It was as though the text of an ancient psalm had been written for her: 'For he shall give his angels charge over thee, to keep thee in all thy ways. They shall bear thee up in their hands, lest thou dash thy foot against a stone.' (Psalm 91: 11, 12).

She heeded this as a warning not to take that path again, and avoided it.
Unfortunately, I do not have the address of this woman, and I was unable to ask her permission to include this story. I hope that she will not mind when she sees that I have immortalized it.

I would now like to continue with a different part of this chapter.

I will begin with the following introduction.
For many years I used to write a story for my family at Christmas. It would be read to the family on Christmas Eve by the light of the Christmas tree.
Since my first book on angels was published, I have sometimes used incidents which really happened as the theme for my story. Afterwards, the family would guess what had really happened, and what I had made up myself.
Here is one of these stories, and this time the reader can guess.

Christmas 1984. Sometimes it seems as though some people are born to fail, while quite the converse applies to others. Some are born under a lucky star; some are dogged by bad luck.
There is no doubt about the category in which Jan Hamer belongs. He was born the son of a farm labourer in Warnsveld. His father was usually drunk, and lived up to his name: he would hammer the whole family to bits when he had been drinking heavily, which was often the case.
His mother bore children, despite her hardships, and Jan, the oldest child, knew her only as a prematurely aged, exhausted and nervous woman. At the turn of the century, when Jan was a child, having a father who was a drunkard meant one thing only: chronic hunger.

Jan was an unappetizing little boy, usually with greenish snot dangling from his nose, and close-cropped hair which was the fashion at the time. When he went outside, a large cap covered his head. He was rather cross-eyed and had suffered from rickets. But although Jan was only a scrap of a boy, he had a secret which he did not share with anyone: he was blessed with a very lively imagination.

From an early age he felt a tremendous hatred for his father. When he was lying in bed at night and heard his father coming home from the pub, and his mother screaming when he beat her up again, his whole body shook with terror, but at the same time he saw himself sitting on a great white horse, dressed in a harness, as he had once seen in a picture, and holding a huge sword in his hand.

He was in the middle of a wood or a forest, and just in front of him he saw a great bully, dragging a woman by the hair. The woman was none other than Grietje from the greengrocer's, who occasionally gave him an apple. With a loud battle-cry he would spur on his horse and strike off the miscreant's head with a tremendous blow. That was the end of the scene, because he was still much too young to imagine what would happen next.

If a child grows up in terrible circumstances, he still often manages to maintain a balance because he simply doesn't know any better. The misery only really began when Jan went to the village school, whose headmaster was Mr Schansema. With the infallible sense which they have for a victim, the children teased Jan mercilessly. The leader of his tormentors was called Harm. He was a great hunk of a boy with a square head, large red hands and a solid, strong body. Harm was Jan's cousin, the son of his father's brother, and as often happens, Harm looked more like Jan's father than Jan himself, who was more like the members of his mother's family. The terrible thing was that Harm knew everything about Jan's circumstances at home, and he referred contemptuously to 'that drunken sot of a father of yours'. He would invent an endless variety of taunts and humiliations. Once he put a wet sponge on Jan's chair, and then loudly cried that Jan had wet his pants. Another time, he waited for Jan outside and would not let him pass when he wanted to go home. Usually it ended in blows, and this was another skill which Harm seemed to have inherited from his uncle, for the blows always landed on target.

At home, Jan could not tell anyone about his misery. 'Have you been fighting again?' his mother would rage when he came home. 'Just wait until I tell your father.' For like so many weak personalities, she took her tormentor's side.

From that time there was a slight change in Jan's fantasies. At the fair he had seen a couple of hussars, and in his imagination, his armour was replaced by a hussar's uniform. The scene of his fantasies was in the school playground. The unknown bully now had a face: it was Harm, and he was dragging Truusje Bakker by the hair. Truusje was the only girl who ever smiled at Jan. Luckily, as a hussar, Jan had a good sized sabre, and soon Harm's head was rolling across the cobbles. Again this was the end of the story, except that sometimes Truusje would stand on her toes and kiss the sturdy hussar on the cheek.

On Sunday mornings, Jan and the whole family went to church. Jan's family belonged to one of the 'heavy' churches, and Sunday after Sunday he would listen to minister Rood preaching fire and brimstone from the pulpit. The minister had red hair, bright green eyes, and a curious high-pitched voice. He delighted in describing the horrors of damnation. Jan was always filled with a deep depression when the violent sermons thundered over him, and when he was about eight years old, he became convinced that he was damned. He must be a terribly bad person, and that was why nobody loved him.

At about this time, his fantasies changed character again. The knight in shining armour and the brave hussar disappeared. Jan started to see quite a different character. It was a shoddily dressed man with a mean grin. Everyone was afraid of him, and it was Jan himself. This was not surprising, because he had become a notorious highwayman – hard on his fellow highwaymen, of whom he was the leader, and merciless to those he robbed.

It was also at this time that he started to realize that a smart boy did not always have to go hungry. He started stealing, and was so good at it that nobody noticed and others were often blamed. This was alright until he was caught one day, stealing a roll from the baker's. He paid heavily for his crime.

The baker gave him a hard clip round the ear, and this was followed by a beating by his father at home, but the worst thing was unexpected. His mother sent him to the minister, who was extremely friendly and understanding, so that Jan burst into tears. For the first time there was an adult who really took an interest in him. For three days he walked round with a feeling of bliss, and the minister was his great hero. Then it was Sunday, and the whole family went to church. To Jan's dismay, the whole sermon was about him. Without mentioning his name, but looking straight at him at regular intervals, the minister preached about a miscreant son who had disgraced his parents. The whole community knew who it was, and glowed with self-righteousness. Then minister Rood ecstatically exclaimed: 'But with tears running down his face, he confessed his sin to me.' At that moment, something froze in Jan. Up to that time, he had felt a great deal of hatred, but his hatred had always been hot. On that Sunday morning, his heart froze and his hatred became icy cold. The highwayman disappeared from his fantasies, and he decided to pay the whole world back for what it had done to him.

But even in this respect, Jan was unlucky. He simply lacked the ability to be a great scoundrel, though he didn't realize this at the time.

In those days children started work when they were very young. Just before Jan left primary school, there was a party at Harm's house because it was Harm's father's birthday.

'What will you do when you leave school?' Jan's aunt asked him. The question seemed friendly enough, but she managed to make it sound as though she thought: 'Probably something fishy.' As the foreman in a brick factory, her husband had done better than Jan's father, and she never missed an opportunity to point this out.

'Not something which makes him throw up,' said Harm. Jan saw no way out of the inevitable humiliation. Once again, Harm was telling the family how Jan had vomited when he had seen a pig slaughtered at the Van Dam's farm. Harm's story went down well, but Jan was glued to his chair, shivering and sweating, for from an early age, he had always felt sick when he saw blood.

Nobody seemed to be really interested about what Jan

wanted to be, although he saw his father giving him a sort of speculative look. He could hardly tell them that he wanted to be a conqueror, first of Warnsveld, then of the province of Gelderland, the Netherlands, and finally the whole of Europe.

On the evening of the day that he was to leave the primary school for good, his father called him and said: 'I suppose you think that you're going to do nothing now, but there's no chance of that; if you don't work, you don't eat.' Then he gave him a note with an address in Zutphen, and said: 'Tomorrow morning, present yourself there. It's an hour's walk, and you have to be there at six o'clock. So get up at quarter to five!'

His father seemed to be secretly laughing.

'What am I going to do there?' Jan asked, rather fearfully.

'That's a surprise', said his father.

It was a beautiful summer's morning as Jan walked to Zutphen. Blackbirds and golden orioles were singing in the beech wood, there were deer grazing in a field in the cool morning air, and two storks flew by overhead. The day seemed to be full of promise. It was as though the tight feeling which was always in his muscles relaxed a little. In Zutphen, he found the right street after looking for a while. The house where he had to present himself turned out to be a large building with wide doors. Above the doors were letters carved in stone which read: City Abattoir.

Jan felt all the blood draining from his face, and he was filled with panic. He wanted to run away, but it was too late. A great brute of a man with little piercing piggy eyes and a low forehead, as hairy as a gorilla, stood by the doorway and started to laugh. Jan recognized him as one of his father's drinking companions.

'Hey! Here's Jan!' he shouted. He grabbed Jan by the arm and took him through the doorway to the large central courtyard. There were cattle tied up everywhere. They walked into a large hall where there were a number of men wearing rubber aprons, dripping with blood.

'Men, this is Jan, who can't stand the sight of blood. He's come to help us,' roared the man who had taken him in. Everyone cheered, and before he knew what was happening to him, all his clothes were ripped off him, and the gorilla was holding him upside down above a tank full of pig's blood. Next to the tank there was a large stone table with at least six slaughtered pigs on it. Other dead pigs were being taken away in small carts.

'One, two, there we go,' called the gorilla, and pushed his head down into the tank. To Jan it was as though time had started moving very slowly. He saw the red surface coming towards him in slow motion, and then his head was submerged in the warm, slippery substance. When he surfaced, he threw up copiously, to the great amusement of the onlookers. Immediately they put a hose on him, and washed him clean.

When he had his clothes back on, he was led to a stone table and they explained what he had to do. He had to remove the eyes of the dead pigs with a sort of button-hook. From that day on, this skinny cross-eyed boy was busy removing eyes. Six days out of seven, he carried out this monotonous and grisly job.

'I will give your wages to your father,' said the gorilla. It soon became clear what this meant. The family was just as poor and hungry as ever, but his father drank even more than before.

It was just after he had been submerged in the pigs' blood that something strange happened to Jan. He had had the feeling before that he was not alone, but it had only been a vague feeling, and had not lasted long. However, now he could clearly feel that there was a 'presence' on his left. This invisible companion never said anything, and yet it was as though Jan could hear his thoughts. What this companion said was both disquieting and exciting.

'It's not true what they've told you,' said the thoughts. 'God doesn't exist. God was made up by the minister. There's only one god, and that's you yourself. Your fate, and that of everyone around you, is in your hands. If you wanted, you could kill everyone, just like the pigs which are slaughtered here, and the first one you could kill is the gorilla.'

Thus, Jan grew up a lonely, brooding, sombre young man. His fear of blood was curiously transformed into a lust for blood. In his few free hours on a Sunday, he would go poaching. Hares, rabbits, birds, and even the occasional deer were among his prey. When he cut the animals' throats, the blood would run over his hands, which he found both grisly, and at the same time, exciting.

When he was fourteen years old, three things happened that changed his life.

His father fell off a cart in a drunken stupor, and was killed outright. Jan went to the funeral, but felt only a slight sense of surprise. It meant that he was the main breadwinner, and that the gorilla had to reluctantly pay him his own wages.

The second important event was the birth of a sister, three months after his father's death. When Jan held the little creature in his arms, something strange happened to him. He felt an overwhelming protective love well up in him for the helpless baby. To himself, he said: 'I could kill someone for you.' The third thing that happened was his encounter with minister Rood senior, the preacher's father. Now that he had retired, he had moved into a cottage in Warnsveld because he wanted to be closer to his son and his family. He was a friendly old man, with white hair, a gold eyeglass, a white moustache and a white goatee. He usually wore a three-piece suit, and his gold watch chain always hung over his waistcoat. It was soon clear that he looked so dapper because his wife did everything for him. The old minister Rood was a very unworldly man who looked at the world with some surprise, and was convinced that everyone was essentially well-intentioned. His son had clearly inherited his mother's fierce nature, and although no one in the community realized it, his hellfire sermons were very similar to the scenes he had witnessed at home as a child when his father once again gave half of his meagre salary to some poor – and, according to his wife – undeserving soul. One day, Jan heard his mother say of the old minister: 'That is how I imagine God.'

From that moment he hated the old man. It was strange, but he no longer hated the gorilla. In fact, he even admired his brutal hardness. He did not hate the minister, for in retrospect, he enjoyed the minister's descriptions of hell. Nor did he hate Harm – on the contrary. Now that he was bigger and stronger, he even tried to be more like Harm. It was as though all the hatred he had ever felt had finally found the perfect target in the figure of this old, unworldly minister. It was not a blazing hatred,

such as that he had felt for his father, but an ice-cold
hatred. It was the cold contempt for an old man he considered to be weak and spineless. Sometimes, when he
cut the throat of a rabbit caught in his snare, he imagined
that he had caught the old minister, and that it was the
latter's blood running over his hands. By now, Jan had
been promoted in the slaughterhouse, and was allowed
to slaughter animals himself. He had grown into a tall,
sinewy boy who was known as 'cross eyes' by everyone.
At first, he had not liked this, but now he considered that
it was part of him.

When Jan was seventeen, he was caught poaching. The
gamekeeper overpowered him in a fight and he went to
prison for six months, for in those days the punishment
for poaching was severe. To his enormous irritation, the
old minister visited him regularly. The old man didn't
seem to realize that he was unwelcome.

He talked quietly of village news, spoke about God, and
always brought something nice to eat with him. Apart
from Jan's mother, he was the only person who visited
the boy, and the more Jan saw him, the more he hated
him – from his mild, rather absent-minded manner, to
his ridiculous watch-chain. Yet he never said anything
unpleasant, and always thanked the minister politely for
the food he had brought.

When he finally came out of prison, he had lost his job.
'We don't need jailbirds here,' said the gorilla. But later
Jan heard that another boy had been employed, whose
money was personally managed by the gorilla.

Jan left prison on his eighteenth birthday, on 17 November, but nobody wanted to employ a boy with his past.
It looked as though Christmas would be dismal, and the
only ray of sunshine was his youngest sister, Maartje,
who was almost four years old and seemed to have no
objection to a brother who had been in prison.

It was almost a week before Christmas when Jan
was called by the old minister. He stood looking around
him rather uncomfortably in the old man's study. The
minister was wearing a dressing gown and was surrounded by more books than Jan had ever seen in one
place.

'Sit down, Jan,' said the minister. 'I want to ask you
something. I have to go to Zutphen once a week, but I

have a cold. You see, I have to get money from the bank, but my wife doesn't want me to go out. Would you get that money for me, if I pay you? I have a cheque here which will authorise you to do that. Next week, I'll be better, and I'll walk there myself because I always enjoy the walk.'

'Yes, minister,' said Jan. As usual, he was extremely quiet when he was with this man, for he saw him as representing everything he despised and hated. As he walked out of the house, he heard the old man's wife shrilly scolding him: 'Now what are you up to? Don't you know that boy's a criminal? How can you trust him with all that money?' Jan stopped a moment to listen, and heard the minister answer: 'If no one trusts him, he won't trust himself in the end. Just leave it to me.' Jan could not remain standing in the hall, and so he walked out of the house as quietly as possible. But he had learnt something interesting. It seemed that the old man was a match for his wife when he needed to be. This gave him a formidable side in Jan's eyes. It was as though one of the rabbits he had trapped suddenly turned out to have tusks. The minister suddenly seemed rather frightening, and this further increased his hatred. But he picked up the money, as he had been asked, and gave it to the minister, every last penny.

Two days before Christmas, Maartje suddenly fell ill. The doctor came and prescribed a medicine, but in the night her condition worsened, and the next day she was groaning. Her head was bent right back and she could not recognize anyone. When the doctor came back, he shook his head sadly, and said that she had an illness which could not be cured. 'I don't think she will last until the evening,' he said. He left the family devastated.

Jan felt overcome by a fury such as he had never experienced before. Until two o'clock in the afternoon he stayed with his mother by the panting child's bedside. The other children were not allowed to come in, for the doctor had said it was contagious. He clearly saw her life slowly ebbing away. Her face had a grey pall, her pupils were large and black, and she breathed in gasps. Her mother was sobbing quietly. Without saying anything, Jan got up and walked out of the back door. He stood still in the little yard.

'You don't have to take this, do you?' said the invisible companion on his left.

'Well, what should I do then?' he asked angrily.

'Get a clever doctor from Zutphen, one from the hospital. That stupid family doctor doesn't know everything,' said his companion.

'That sort of thing is only for the rich. I haven't got any money,' snarled Jan.

'Get some money then,' said his companion.

'Where from?' he asked curtly. 'Does it grow on trees?'

'It certainly does,' said his companion. 'Today it's growing in the pocket of old minister Rood. He's walking back from Zutphen this afternoon, after getting money from the bank.'

'And will he just give it to me?' asked Jan, but he knew the answer even before he had heard it.

'No, but you've got your axe. His life's almost over anyway, and if he really looks like God, you can pay Him back for all the tricks he's played on you. It's your chance to kill two birds with one stone. What's more, that'll give you the money to pay for the doctor for your sister.'

Jan nodded, and walked to the shed. It was as though his whole life had been moving towards this moment. Suddenly the dam broke, and a tidal wave of hatred began to move in the direction of the unsuspecting old man.

'Which path will he take?' asked Jan, getting the sharp axe from the shed.

'Not the main road, but the path through the woods,' said the companion. His voice was almost as clear as that of a real person – a cold, businesslike voice.

'When will he be there?' asked Jan.

'You've seen him walking back a few times,' said the companion. 'Between four and five o'clock, when it's quite dark.'

'Will Maartje be dead by then?' asked Jan.

'We'll see about that. One thing at a time.'

Jan walked along the path through the woods to Zutphen, the axe hidden in a sack. Halfway, there was some heathland with a few fir trees. It was a wintry day, and the frozen ground crackled under his feet. He hid behind the fir trees and waited to see what would happen. Something in him said: 'If he doesn't come past, he's meant to live. Otherwise, I'll kill him.'

The first stars had come out, and slowly the light of the rising moon was becoming stronger. A deer crossed the heathland, nibbled on a bush, suddenly pricked up its ears, and sprang quickly back into the woods.

Jan clearly heard footsteps on the path, coming from the direction of Zutphen. He took out his axe and the metal glinted coldly in the moonlight. He wondered whether the blood of such an old man would spurt out in the same way as that of a pig.

Suddenly he felt his companion moving. He had always been on the left, but now he left his place and flowed into Jan's body on the left side. He felt an enormous ruthless force overpowering him. Even if he had wanted to do anything else, this was no longer possible. His muscles were like cables, full of terrible strength. His thoughts were utterly single-minded and aimed at his approaching prey.

Then he saw him, the old minister. He was walking slowly through night with a black hat on his head, the white moustache and goatee shining in the moonlight, but he was not alone. Two sturdy farmer's boys walked on his left and right. They were wearing faded smocks and trousers, and wore caps on their flaxen hair. Their yellow clogs glinted in the moonlight.

As soon as Jan saw the two men accompanying the old minister, he felt his companion flowing out of him. It was as though there was a sort of hiss, like the noise of an adder which has been surprised.

The three men walked by the fir trees, and there was Jan, his whole body shaking and shivering, the axe in his quivering hands.

The companion was gone. 'Even he has left me in the lurch,' thought Jan bitterly. Then a new thought entered his mind. He saw the beams in his house, and as clearly as though he were standing there, he saw a rope hanging from those beams, and the body, still jerking, dangling from the rope: his own body.

'Yes', he thought, 'this is the end. I don't want to go on anymore.'

When he went home, it was as though he was surrounded by an infinite silent space. The stars, the moon, the night sky itself, seemed to have withdrawn to an immeasurable distance, and there he was, quite alone, in an empty universe.

When he was almost home, he saw – to his great surprise – that a warm light was shining from the window. He went in, and heard his mother singing gaily, not on her own, but with the other children. Altogether they had started to sing 'Glory to God!' and – what was that? – were his ears deceiving him? – amongst them he heard the unmistakably merry voice of Maartje. At first it was as though he was rooted to the ground. Then he walked into the room, dragging his feet. The room was gaily lit with at least five candles, and decorated with holly and branches of fir trees.

Mother was sitting in a chair by the wood fire with all the children around her, and little Maartje on her lap, crowing with delight. Jan stared at them open-mouthed. For the first time in his life, he noticed that his mother had beautiful warm eyes and a sensitive mouth.

'Mother, what happened?' he stammered.

'Sit down and I'll tell you,' she said.

Very carefully he stroked Maartje's hair and sat down on the floor by his mother's feet.

'When you went,' she said, 'Maartje's breathing became shallower and shallower. From time to time she stopped breathing altogether. Her feet were blue and cold, and I was terribly sad and couldn't stop weeping.

Suddenly, there was a brightly shining apparition next to Maartje's bed. I don't know if it was a man or a woman. The apparition looked at me lovingly, bent forward, and took Maartje out of bed. I saw that it was an angel, and couldn't move a finger. The angel walked off with her, and I sat alone by the empty bed. I said to myself that Maartje had died. But a little later the angel came back, gave me a warm look, and put Maartje back in her bed. Then suddenly he disappeared. I sat absolutely still, and I knew that Maartje was not dead, but that she had been cured! I looked at her carefully, and saw that she was looking at me. Then she said: 'Mummy, I'm thirsty.' The doctor has been. He was completely bowled over. He said that he'd never come across anything like it, and that it was a miracle.'

It was as though the old crust of ice, which had always

surrounded Jan's heart, started to melt. He covered his face with his hands, and started weeping passionately for the first time in his life. No one looked at the clock, but it's said that he cried for two hours while the rest of the family sat around him and stroked him.

At last the sobs ceased, he removed his hands from his face, and looked at his mother. He saw her eyes growing large and round with amazement. All the others also looked at him, and it was suddenly very quiet in the room.

'What is it?' he asked. 'What's the matter with me?'

Then Maartje burst out laughing, pointing at him, and everyone else laughed as well. His mother cried: 'Jan, Jan, you're no longer cross-eyed.'

He stood up and walked to the hall.

He looked in the mirror, and his eyes looked straight back. Then he said slowly: 'So God does exist, and He loves us.'

When Jan got up the next day, he noticed that for the first time since he had been submerged in the pig's blood, he was alone. The invisible companion had disappeared. When he came outside, the world looked as though it had been newly created. It had matured, and all the trees and bushes were shrouded in incredibly fine lace. The very sky sparkled, as though it had just been made.

He walked into the village, and almost automatically, his steps took him to the old minister's house. For a while he stood deep in thought; then he rang the bell. The minister opened the door himself.

'Ah, Jan, come in, come in. How nice to see you. What! You're no longer cross-eyed. How can that be?'

Jan sat down and said:

'Minister, I must tell you something terrible.'

'Go ahead, my boy. We are alone here. My wife has just gone into the village, so no one can disturb us.'

'Minister, yesterday you were coming back from Zutphen after getting the money from the bank . . .' said Jan.

'So I was,' laughed the old man. 'My wife was angry when I came home. She said that in the dark, the path through the woods is much too dangerous for an old man with a lot of money on him.'

'Minister,' said Jan, 'she was quite right.' He looked down at the ground, cleared his throat, and said:
'I was standing there with an axe, ready to murder you and take your money. If those two men hadn't happened to be walking with you, you would have been dead now!'
'What men do you mean?' asked the minister in surprise.
'Well, those two peasant boys wearing clogs, walking on your left and right. They were big strong lads, and there was absolutely no chance that I could hurt you in any way.'
The old preacher was silent for a little while. Then he said:
'My friend, I walked alone the whole way, but it is clear to me what happened. God sent His angels to protect me and you.'
How did this story about Jan end?
It had a happy ending. With the help of his old friend, minister Rood senior, he became the gamekeeper on a large estate near Zutphen. In his spare time, he did a lot of good visiting young offenders in special schools in the vicinity. It was said that there were few people who were so good at putting young people who had strayed, back on the right path. He married a loving wife, no less than Truusje Bakker, the only girl who had smiled at him when he was at primary school.
Maartje became a nurse. She says that she remembers how the angel took her with him, but she never told anyone where she went.
When the old minister told his wife what had happened, swearing her to secrecy, she said: 'Didn't I tell you that you shouldn't walk along that dangerous path in the woods on your own? Let that be the last time!'
From then on, minister Rood junior fetched the money for his father from Zutphen once a week, and the old man was truly sorry about this, for he was very fond of the heath in the moonlight.

Now I will ask the reader the same thing I asked my family after reading this story on Christmas Eve: which part of the story is true?
Here is the answer.
You will have noticed that there are actually two stories woven together. The development of Jan, culminating in

attempted murder and being saved from that, and Maartje's illness, culminating in her recovery.

The parts of the story about Jan which are literally true are these:

9 The old minister really lived. He was the grandfather of the man who told me his story. The story took place in the neighbourhood of Zutphen at the turn of the century. The retired minister was very fond of walking along the path through the woods to Zutphen, but his wife was rather cross with him, for she thought it was much too dangerous when he had a great deal of money on him.

One day he was visited by a man, who told him that he had been converted and that he wished to confess a sin. The minister was then told the story about the two men who were accompanying him, and about the murder which did not happen.

The parts I added are the description of Jan's character, how he became the person he was, what he felt like, etc. The story about the cure of his astigmatism is also invented, but I was inspired by many of the miraculous cures which I have witnessed in Jerusalem in the services of Kathryn Kuhlman. Jan's appearance: the sinewy, cross-eyed man, and his job, removing the eyes of dead pigs, were taken from a different source. During our training as reserve officers, we had to visit the pig abattoirs in Oss.

We saw how the pigs were first administered an anaesthetizing electric shock, were then pulled up by their hind legs with a rope, and then the aorta was cut. The blood flowed into a tank, and then the cadavers were taken through an enormous hall along rails attached to the ceiling. The pigs were hung from these rails by their hind legs. First they were submerged in hot water, then they passed through a big fire, and then they were passed slowly past the factory workers, who each performed one particular step. It was there that I saw the sinewy, cross-eyed man who did just one thing all day long, and that was to take out the eyes with a sort of large hook. He was wearing a rubber apron, and between his legs there was pyramid of peeled eyes.

When we had watched the whole procedure, we were offered a piece of smoked sausage, which half of the doctors thoroughly enjoyed eating. This is where I got my description of Jan.

I described minister Rood's wife as being rather more fierce than she really was; the poor woman was simply worried.

The description of the angels is not quite right either. I described them as farm labourers, but in reality they were only referred to as men.

The description of Jan's wish to commit suicide is taken from an analogous case in my practice.

Jan's character reveals clear signs of being possession. No one should imagine that this no longer exists; I have seen possessed people several times.

Now Maartje's story.

This moving story is true, but comes from another source. It took place in the north of the Netherlands, a little later in the twentieth century.

10 One day a woman asked her mother-in-law: 'You have four children and you love them all equally . . . yet I have the feeling that there is a special bond between you and your youngest daughter. Is that true?' Then the mother-in-law told her that she had guessed correctly and went on to explain how the youngest daughter had become dreadfully ill when she was a toddler and had been given up for dead by the doctor. From then on, the events happened exactly as described in my Christmas story. The angel really took the child out of her bed, and really brought her back. I made up the illness because I do not know what was the matter with the child. There is a reason why I combined the stories about minister Rood and Maartje, but I will come back to that later. Lastly, I ought to add that the true character of the child's mother did not correspond in any way to that of Maartje's mother, who was a downtrodden and battered woman. I described her character in that way because it was necessary for the story.

The reason why I included my Christmas story in this book is this.

Several times we have seen how two eyewitnesses saw one angel. This time we have the opposite situation, viz., two angels seen by one person.

This phenomenon of the 'two angels' occurs repeatedly. The double angel runs through my archives like a red thread. In my first book I gave an example of it in the story of 'Happy Breet'.

11 One of the earliest stories in this genre can be found in the book *In het uur der bezinning* (In the Hour of Reflection) by A.M. Lindeboom, who describes how a minister was protected in 1880 by two 'men', when a gang of thugs wished to hurt him one evening as he was walking along a dark road. The minister did not see his protectors, but the thugs did, and one of them later told the minister about this.

12 Lindeboom tells another story like this, about the evangelist Haitsma from Vledderveen, who was protected by two shining figures from ruffians who wished to murder him. Again, only the attackers saw the figures. The evangelist saw nothing.

13 The earliest story of this type was written down in Middelburg in 1700, about a minister called Smytegelt. This is described in the *Noord– en Zuidnederlandse Sagen* (Sagas of the Northern and Southern Netherlands), Willem Hofman, Elsevier 1974. In my first book I included another story about two angels which took place in South Africa, where they prevented a man from being attacked by highwaymen.

14 In Drente, minister J. van Petegem once preached so vehemently against alcohol abuse, that visits to the local pubs declined considerably. The publicans decided to eliminate the minister. They watched him closely for a while, and noticed that he always went to a meeting in the area on the same evening every week. To go there he had to cross a little bridge over a marsh. It was decided to throw him into the marsh as he was crossing the bridge, and to leave him to drown.
The men who wanted to murder him could not do anything because of the protection which accompanied the minister.
However, they were not sinners who confessed to their intentions, as in other stories. They were quite mad, went

to visit minister van Petegem in the rectory and
demanded furiously: 'Who betrayed us? In recent weeks
you have always walked alone on that evening, and just
when we want to do you in, there were two men walking
with you.'
Van Petegem had not seen anything, and realized
straightaway who they had been.
Finally – without wishing to become monotonous – there
is the following story.

15 There was a simple, devout man who did many
good deeds. He was a sort of inventor, and he had
patented an invention relating to windmills. As a result,
he unexpectedly earned a lot of money, and this aroused
the envy of his competitors. One day, when he was
coming back from a church council meeting, some of
these jealous men were waiting for him. It was a dark
night, and they wanted to throw him into a ditch. But
they were unable to do so because there were two hefty
men accompanying him. Later, the men confessed to him
what they had intended to do, and he said: 'They must
have been angels, for I was just thinking about
God.'
Here then, is the explanation which I still owe you. The
last man, the inventor, was the grandfather of the woman
who asked her mother-in-law about the special relationship she had with her youngest daughter.
Thus you could say that in that woman's family there are
angels on both sides of the family. This is where the
association in my Christmas story came from. So
altogether there are eight of these analogous stories,
stretching from 1700 to the present day, and from Africa
to the Netherlands.
It is interesting to compare these eight stories. There is a
clear pattern:
(1) a preacher/devout man/evangelist
(2) in danger of falling victim to attempted murder
(3) for his preaching/devout deeds/money
(4) is awaited on a dark night,
(5) but the attempt fails
(6) because there are two men/shining figures, walking
with him
(7) and although he does not see them himself,

(8) he finds out because his attackers confess to him or to someone else
(9) and he realizes that angels have saved him.

A number of factors become apparent. We note the following correspondences:
1. The succession of events is always the same, as described above.
2. The person to be attacked is always a devout man.
3. The attack is always planned to take place at night.
4. There are always two angels (although minister Lindeboom mentions one analogous case with one angel).
5. It is always the attackers who see the angels.
6. The source of the information, although very often closely related to the victim (grandchild, great-grandchild) is never the victim him or herself (except,

All this can be summarized in a table as follows:

TIME	PLACE	VICTIM	ATTACKER	NUMBER OF ATTACKERS	METHOD OF ATTACK	NUMBER OF ANGELS	SOURCE OF INFORMATION	MADE AVAILABLE BY
1700	Middle-burg	Priest Father Smyte-geld	?	?	?	2	Holman (book)	?
1880	Zaandam	Priest	rough men	?	?	2	Father Lindeboom	?
19th century	Africa	Priest	robbers	2	in the wilderness	2	great grand-daughter	publican
19th/ 20th century	Den Helder	Baker Breet	pimp	2	drowning by bridge	2	acquaintance of family	book by Breet
19th/ 20th	Vledder-veen	Haitsma evangelist	drunkard	2	heath	2	Father Lindeboom	confession
19th/ 20th century	Eefde	preacher	robber	1	heath	2	grandson	confession
19th century	?	inventor	competitors	2 or 3	drowning in ditch	2	grand-daughter	confession
20th century	Drent	Priest Father van Petegem	publican	2 or 3	drowning in marsh	2	letter	confession

perhaps, in the case of Breet, who wrote the story down himself). Personally I have never spoken to anyone who actually had this sort of angel experience themselves. However, Mr. Lindeboom has.

7. In all the cases, the victim is mentioned by name and the place is given.

In addition, there are some striking aspects, though these are not common to every case:

a. Three attempts at drowning, two of which took place by a bridge.

b. Three times people feel that their livelihood is threatened by the devout man.

c. Three times the story is told by a direct descendant.

Is this comparable to the 'angel by the motorway'?

In other words, is this a 'monkey roll' story which covers almost three centuries in the various versions? Despite the fact that I have not spoken to any direct eyewitnesses, I still feel that I should strongly deny this.

In every case, the person involved and the place where the incident occurred are precisely known. Number 7 is an exception as regards the place, but my correspondent forgot to mention where the grandfather lived. Moreover, in four of the eight cases, I am personally acquainted with the sources of the information about the double angel.

The main reason why I do not think that these are 'monkey roll' stories is based on previous experiences.

There is nothing more accurate than a good family story. I come from a family in which many stories are told about distant forefathers, and whenever it is possible to check on these, they always turn out to be correct. It is as though an ancient human ability has survived in family stories, viz., that of oral tradition, on which our distant forefathers relied totally.

When two grandchildren and a great-granddaughter of men who had a double angel experience describe this story to me personally as part of their family tradition, I believe that there is a 99% probability that the story is based on truth.

If this is the case, why are the stories so similar?

Perhaps they are so alike because they reflect a universal truth.

I am not talking here about the fact that guardian angels

save people. That does not go far enough. We should never forget that experiences of angels are not part of our ordinary everyday world. They are closer to the world of our dreams, the world of nighttime, and therefore they have a symbolic value as well as their literal value – in this case, of saving someone.

Just consider the fact that almost all the attacks took place at night, or at least in the dark. In itself, this is an indication of the other side of the world, the side of which we are not aware when we are wide awake. People who are firmly rooted in this outside world think that they have to organize everything themselves in that world. Those who have links with the other side know better. These people do not have to organize things feverishly, but can trust in God, and often experience miracles. Chinese philosophers spoke of "sitting still, doing nothing", which did not mean being lazy, but indicated a connection with the quiet side of existence. The same principle is expressed in Psalm 127:2, where it says: 'It is vain for you to rise up early, to sit up late, to eat the bread of sorrows; for so he giveth his beloved sleep.'

It is striking that in all eight stories the devout man is actually passive. He is "thinking about God" or "enjoying a walk over the moors by moonlight". Breet comes back from a failed attempt at doing good. And all these people, who live a fairly passive life, are attacked by active, devious robbers or other scoundrels. Then we see how the miracle takes place: violent men are impotent against those protected by God. They are defeated by the person who does not resort to violence. This is a very ancient phenomenon. Violent men believe that the world moves round them, and that they are the ones who make history. Nothing could be further from the truth. True decisions are made by the attitudes of quiet, peaceful people in whom there is no violence. A city may be surrounded by the enemy. Everything seems hopeless. Then the city is relieved. Was there a stronger army in that city? No, one or two 'just' people lived there, people who were almost unknown, but the city was saved by and for them.

These quiet people who are in tune with God, not only know about this world and its noise, bustle of activity, violence and calculated scheming. They are also aware of the other side, where one good deed puts the world on a different track. It is precisely because they know about 'the other side' that there are little bridges in these eight stories, and it is exactly on one of these bridges where the evil deed is planned that people are saved.

In these eight stories the number '2' plays an obstinate role. There are two attackers, two angels, a story passed down to us through two generations, two shores connected to each other. In addition to concentrating on the way in which people are saved by angels, these stories insist that we should not forget the other side! At a time when materialism has started to prevail, and an understanding of the other world has become increasingly veiled, these stories tell us about this world *and* the other world, heaven *and* earth. We should not forget either of them, but link them together like the bridge which joined the two banks.

Let us take a closer look at the two angels.

There is an old Jewish tradition that everyone is always flanked by two angels. The angel on the right is a source of inspiration to do good, and the angel on the left keeps count of the mistakes that we make, not to inflict punishment, but to put someone in a situation where he can rectify his mistakes.

Could it be that the attackers do not see two hastily drummed up angels, but that their eyes are opened for a moment so that they are able to perceive the permanent situation?

I do not know whether this hypothesis is correct, but at least it reveals two sides of the question.

The person who was threatened is saved, and in many cases his attackers are put on the right track.

This course of events is so characteristic of God's way that I see the vicar with the two angels as an integral part of the mosaic of stories about angels.

It is actually easy to miss the essential aspect, for a person can be saved in such a spectacular way that we tend only to think about the way in which the devout man was saved. However, the essential point is the way in which the evil man is saved. At worst, the vicar would have lost his life. But the evil man could have done irreparable damage to his immortal soul. We are not concerned primarily with the way in which physical bodies are saved, but with the salvation of the immortal soul. That is why devout people are often used in the great plan of salvation without being aware of it.

In the "double angel" stories, there are two stories side by side:

1. The devout man is attacked and saved from death.
2. The evil man is given a shock, confesses his sins, and is converted.

If I have understood the Bible correctly, the emphasis is on the second story. It is above all the scoundrels who are saved. Later we will come across events which are quite similar to the above-mentioned stories, but the devout man with the double angel is so special that he deserves a place of honour in this book. He reminds us of the great plan for this world: salvation.

I can well imagine that a twentieth century person feels rather uncomfortable about my proposition that the angels who are seen by the scoundrels are always with us. One might suppose that this meant that there are always two figures rather shiftily creeping alongside us. In a cathedral you may have noticed a painting of an enormous eye looking down on you from above. This is God's all-seeing eye. I do not find the sensation of this eye altogether pleasant. We twentieth century people like to do everything ourselves, and don't like the idea that there is someone looking over our shoulder. Just imagine being constantly aware of two figures, one on either side of you. What would you do? What would you omit to do? Would this knowledge be a help or a hindrance? Would we crawl into our shells, or would our wings grow even stronger? I am deliberately stating this in a rather absurd way because I believe that this way of think- ing misses the point.

There is another aspect of the double angel story which deserves attention, and that is the following: three times the story was passed down by an older generation. Twice I was told the story by a grandchild, and once by the great-grandchild of the person concerned. I have already said that this is a very strong argument for the story being true, but it also has a symbolic significance. Who are our grandparents? They play a very different role from our parents. Our parents bring us into this world. They make sure that we manage here as well as possible. They represent the daytime side of our existence.

Our grandparents not only connect us with the past of our own family, but also with the past of mankind as a whole. Mum tests us on our homework; Granny tells fairytales. Dad teaches us skills; Grandad teaches us wisdom (if things are as they should be). When a person died in the Old Testament, it was said that he was "gathered unto his forefathers". This did not mean a Jewish cemetery, but a return to the oneness of life, which has broken down here on earth.

Hopefully the story about the double angel comes to us from our ancestors – in this way we learn to put those angels in perspective. Look at a small boy going for a walk with his grandfather. The boy is still close to heaven, whence he has just come, and the grandfather is close to heaven, because he will not be here very long. They enjoy each other because they feel closer because of heaven than parents and children feel.

This should be our viewpoint when we consider the double angel. They are the rungs of a ladder to heaven, as familiar as our grandparents, safe and friendly and not pushy in any way. The double angel is our double certainty that God means us well.

The two angels should be just as familiar to us as our two eyes. After all, we do not feel spied upon just because our eyes always look with us. In fact, they allow us to see. The two angels are just as close to us as our ears. Isn't it wonderful that these two unbelievably finely tuned organs listen with us? Sometimes we can have a ringing in our ears, and it is only then we realize what a blessing it is that our ears are usually quiet. The two angels which God has given us are just as quiet and modest.

Let us be glad of the lesson taught in these eight stories: we are looked after better than we imagined in our wildest dreams.

CHAPTER 2

ANGELS AT SEA AND IN THE AIR

W.W. Jacobs, an unparalleled story teller from the beginning of this century, often tells his comic stories through the medium of picturesque characters: an old man begging for a beer in a village cafe or a night watchman with beady eyes standing on the quayside. The latter, who has many stories about seamen, is wont to say: "Everyone is superstitious . . . . superstition: that's all very well, up to a certain extent but, as always, some people go too far, of course. They have a hole in the head."

Then he tells the story of two seamen who had sworn a solemn oath that the first to die would visit the other one to prove that there was a hereafter. At a certain moment the first sailor actually does visit the other one in the middle of the night with some seaweed on his head to show that he has been drowned. The other one is frightened to bits and is pressed to pay a lot of money to the widow of the drowned sailor. It is quite clear that this is not a spirit from another world but a leg-pull, although the sailor who was tricked never finds out.

I could imagine that after reading the stories about angels in this book one might be inclined to say: "Do you believe everything you are told? Isn't that rather naïve?"

This is a serious and difficult question.

If an experience of angels is shared by two or more people

it has more credibility than if only one person is involved. This is not because that one person is less reliable, but because two witnesses can confirm a story. For example, the angel child who saved the toddler from being run over was seen by the toddler's father and her mother, and therefore the evidence for a true story about angels is stronger than the story about the mother who saw the angel leaving the room with her sick child.

This is the case, even though we know that a miracle had occurred in the story about the sick child. One witness is actually one witness too few. Thus it is also easier to assume that the story about the woman on the escalator is true because her husband confirmed it, than to believe the story of the woman who told the story about a dematerialised lorry driving straight through her car, because she was alone. This is unfortunate for her for she is a very reliable woman but there is something missing in her story. Unfortunately, we do not have an account of this incident from the driver of the oncoming lorry.

This problem always arises when a story is told by just one man or woman. At the time that rumours were circulating about angels on the motorway, I was telephoned by someone from the KRO radio station who asked me whether I would comment on this phenomenon in a live broadcast. I was asked an interesting question:

"Can the existence of angels be proved scientifically?"

What is scientific proof? In science we have arrived at some agreements to establish what does and what does not count as scientific proof.

One of these agreements is that something can only be satisfactorily studied and proved if it can be repeated. If I see one hundred times over that water freezes when the temperature drops below 0°C., then I can put forward the scientific hypothesis that the freezing point of water is 0°C. Anyone who wishes to try this will find the same freezing point – unless there are many salts dissolved in the water, in which case the freezing point is lower.

With angels it is difficult to ask them to come back the next day because you want to prove their existence scientifically. Thus, because of the restrictions we have imposed on the definition of scientific proof, an angel cannot be scientifically proved to exist in our century. On the other hand, if we were to agree that other criteria applied to the experiences of angels than those which we use for our material world, we would certainly find that it would be possible to establish with a degree of probability bordering on certainty that angels do exist and can intervene in our lives.

In this chapter I started with the night watchman on the quayside, for now it is the turn of sailors. During the t.v. programme which I made with Sonja, mentioned in the last chapter, a sailor told a wonderful story. Television programmes are shortlived and soon forgotten, and that is why I would like to record his astonishing experience.

16 A ship laden with a cargo of wood was ploughing through a storm. The waves rolled in on the starboard side and disappeared under the violently rocking ship to the port side. On that side, on the left of the ship, there was a sailor. Behind him there was a large cargo of wood. Suddenly an enormous wave rolled in, the ship turned through ninety degrees, the wood started to move and crashed into the sea with a thundering crash, dragging the poor sailor with it. Suddenly he found himself under water with the whole cargo of wood above him and he knew that his last hour was at hand. All of a sudden he saw a great bright light and in the glow of this light he clearly saw his whole family at home. Then he was lifted up from underneath the wood by a gigantic force and, clearly seen by some of the crew, he was placed on the port side of the ship which had now been righted. Just imagine the situation: he was in the water on the lee side, which means that the waves were rolling away from the ship. Therefore it could not have been a wave which lifted him back on board. No, he was put back on the ship against the direction of the wind and the furious waves.

It is a pity that there was not another member of the crew of that ship to confirm his story during the programme but I don't think it would have been difficult to find one. Once again I am reminded of the difficult question asked by skeptics: "Do you believe everything that people tell you?" I will discuss that question in more detail later on, but first here is another sailor's story.

17 The second mate on a freight ship of the Holland-America Line wrote to me about an experience he had had. In 1936 they were on the point of leaving Philadelphia. It was night time and he just wanted to check that the cargo was properly stowed. He had forgotten to take his torch but as he knew the way like the back of his hand, he did not go back to his cabin to fetch it. First he passed through a dark hole to the so-called spa deck, a deck immediately below the upper deck. To get there he had to go down some stairs in the pitch dark, and as he made his way, he thought that he would be able to see enough with a few matches. Once he had reached the spa deck he walked towards a steel ladder which led to the decks below. The steel ladder was just behind a closed hatch. When he thought he was there, he put his left foot on the hatch and stretched out his hand to take hold of the ladder, but he found that he was stepping into nothingness and fell down forwards, realising to his dismay that the hatch had been opened and that he would probably be smashed to pieces. The hole yawning below him was about nine metres deep. As he plummeted down, scraping one leg along the side of the open hatch, he suddenly saw a figure. It was dressed completely in white, as though it was wearing a white overall which came down over his feet. Although it was still pitch dark he could see the figure quite clearly. Where the eyes and mouth should have been he could only see dark lines.

He immediately thought: this is a guardian angel, a messenger from God, and he shut his eyes in awe. When he opened them, the figure had vanished and the sailor noticed that he was standing on the ladder. From that day he often thought: Why did God save me? Why was I spared? What does God want from me?

For people who want proof, this story is more difficult to believe because it is told by just one man. On the other hand, he gives such precise details about the decks – more than I have described here – and about the exact location where the experience took place, that it is almost as though you were there yourself.

It's true that there is only one witness, but this is a story which feels as true as you could wish. For example, he mentions the detail of covered feet which is a common feature of encounters with angels. In addition there is the description of the angel's face. In a made-up story you would expect more than a vague indication of the eyes and the mouth which could only be seen as dark lines. Finally, there is one other very strong aspect. The man wrote me this story in 1985; in other words, forty-nine years after he had had the experience.

The combination of a memory which had been preserved crystal clear for almost half a century and the down-to-earth description of details, is typical of true experiences. It is worth saying a little more about the letters I receive. At the time that I carried out my angel enquiry I put a sudden question to my patients after their consultations, and asked them if they had ever seen an angel. My first book on angels was written on the basis of their spontaneous responses and their stories. Of course it is essentially quite different when readers subsequently write you letters about experiences they have had, encouraged by that book. These accounts are not spontaneous and the stories could be more easily embellished, changed or even made up. Therefore for skeptical people, the value of these stories which were sent to me could be rather less than those about the experiences which were recounted in answer to my unexpected question after consultations. The letters on which I wrote "True Angels" in thick red letters were therefore selected quite critically. I included only those letters in which the experiences were recounted in an almost businesslike way, in which the story made sense, and in which the details corresponded with reality as far as I could ascertain. In addition, I included only those letters which reveal that the experience had been a spontaneous one. By spontaneous I mean that they had not occurred after meditation exercises, with the use of drugs or under hypnosis.

Despite this strict selection I still had more than one hundred and fifty true angel stories which all contained characteristic aspects of "true stories". They correspond closely with those aspects which I have found to be typical of angel experiences. In many cases they took place in dangerous circumstances or in cases of psychological distress. In the majority of cases there was a sudden appearance and disappearance. In many cases the people involved only realized afterwards what they had experienced. Looking back at the experience, they suddenly realized how extraordinary it had been. Finally the letters also showed, just as I had heard in my surgery, that the people had often remained silent about their experiences for many years, even to their nearest and dearest.

So why do I have so much confidence in the letters which people wrote to me? I will try to explain.

Once someone has been in a profession for a long time, he finally acts with professional feeling. An old carpenter will immediately recognize the right sort of wood to use simply by touching it.

I was once on a board with a former chartered accountant who instantly recognized that there was something fishy about the accounts. Nobody realized it, but he insisted on finding out what was wrong with a particular account. He was proved 100% correct. How did he know this? Throughout the years he had developed an instinct about misleading figures. My father, a public prosecutor, could simply smell whether someone was guilty. "That man is the murderer," he would say with complete certainty. "How do you know that, Dad?" I would ask. He couldn't explain it very well but he was always proved right.

In my own profession I have had to develop an instinct to know whether people are telling the truth. This is very important for a doctor. You can only help someone if you have as much information as possible, but many people fail to mention the most important things not because they want to mislead, but very often because they are ashamed or afraid. The following is an example which illustrates this.

I remember a woman who came to me with terrible eczema. She had been treated by her G.P. for a year and a half, and she was also seeing a psychiatrist because she had become so tense. The psychiatrist had already been treating her for six months.

I asked her whether anything had happened just before the eczema had appeared but she said this was not the case. However, I saw a look in her eyes which gave me the feeling that she was holding something back. When I persisted in asking whether something had happened, she said, "My oldest son started his military service". Then she was silent. I asked whether that was specially

significant for her and she became very emotional. She
told me the following story:

In 1940 she had become pregnant by her fiancé and they
were to be married soon. Then war broke out and her
fiancé was killed at the Grebbe Line, where the Dutch
army fought a great battle against the German troops
marching into the Netherlands. She had a son, and a little
later she met the man to whom she is still married and
with whom she also had several children. It was a good
marriage.

When her oldest son first came home on leave wearing
his uniform, he looked so much like the fiancé who had
died, that it gave her a terrible shock. She suddenly
realised that her love for this first man had not disappeared but that she still loved him, and her conscience
troubled her greatly about her present husband. She felt
confused and guilty. I explained to her that her feelings
about the first man in her life were quite normal and that
it was even a good thing that she still had those feelings.
She was tremendously relieved that she had finally told
someone about it and that she was not hurting her present
husband.

Then I asked her: "You have already been seeing a psychiatrist for six months. Why did you never tell him
about this?" She answered: "Oh, doctor, he is a psychiatrist in the marine hospital and when I saw the jacket
of his uniform hanging on the door I couldn't tell him
about it". It is strange details like these which determine
whether a patient tells you what matters, or not. Her
eczema actually cleared up in a fortnight.

Therefore, I feel confident about the letters I received,
because of the ability to recognise the truth which I have
learned in the course of the years.

People who consciously tell you made-up stories are
extremely rare. As I have just explained, people often fail
to relate information for all sorts of reasons, but hardly
anyone tells totally imaginary tales.

Therefore, I believe that the 150 experiences about angels
which I have carefully selected are reasonably reliable
and are good enough for the anthology contained in this
book.

If we come across angels at sea, what about angels in the
air, or in space . . . ? Or you could say: if we see angels

floating on water, aren't they all the more to be expected in the air?

The sky, by definition, is quite different from heaven, which is not above us but round the corner. But nevertheless, it is significant that we use the same word for the blue heaven above and God's heaven: there is a relationship between them. Let us take to the air like true members of the twentieth century. We will start in a light-hearted vein. A strange photograph has been circulating in the Netherlands which was allegedly taken like this:

18 In July 1984, a woman from Chicago flew to Texas. The flight took several hours. For a long time she could see the enormous Mississippi River meandering far below. During the flight there was a terrible thunderstorm and the plane shook and trembled.

A thunderstorm seen from a plane is quite different from a storm seen on the ground. Standing on earth you see a leaden sky with occasional flashes of lightning coming down, but from a plane it is as though the clouds are lit up from inside with a bright white light. It is a fantastic sight to fly along these towering masses of clouds which are lit up from inside in all sorts of fantastic shapes. But it is by no means impossible or unlikely that the plane could be wrecked. Thus the travellers were extremely frightened, the plane shuddered and shook and many people started praying out loud.

The woman from Chicago was sitting by a window and seemed to have nerves of steel, for she found the spectacle outside so fascinating that she took a photograph.

Fortunately the trip ended happily. Everyone arrived in Texas unhurt. However, when the photograph was developed, the lady from Chicago made a strange discovery. Outside the plane you could see the gigantic figure of someone dressed in white. It looked most like a man in a white habit tied with a dark belt. It had white sleeves and above the darker neck there was a vague outline of the head. The cloud swirled around his figure. The figure and the cloud could clearly be seen against an inky black background.

Before I say anything else about this photograph I will tell you that there is something strange about this story.

According to an equally reliable seeming report, this incident actually took place over the sea between Australia
and New Zealand. Apparently the lady who took the
photograph told the story to a vicar, Mr. Powson. One
detail lacking in the first version, is that during the terrible
storm the woman asked her neighbour whether she was
a Christian. When she answered in the affirmative, the
women prayed together to ask if Jesus could still
the storm just as he had done on the Sea of Galilee. The
photograph was taken just after the prayer.

Thus, we have a strange situation that there is only one
photograph – and there is no doubt about that because it
is lying in front of me – but there are two versions of
the story. You could call the two versions the "business
version" and the "Christian version". This is one of the
rather irritating aspects of heavenly matters. They are
never quite logically consistent.

For example, Our Lord had one life but the four writers
of the Gospels all wrote their own versions. These versions do not contradict each other much (although they
are sometimes contradictory) but rather support and
complement each other. I always compare them to a
gigantic tree. Four people standing at the four points of
the compass will write four different descriptions of this
one tree.

Is it possible to photograph an angel? The photograph
looks real, but I am no expert. Is it really possible? If we
can see an angel why shouldn't it be possible to record it
on photographic paper? But why didn't the woman see
anything when she took the photograph?

There is something shocking about an angel on a photograph. It seems rather profane. Perhaps we all have – an
admittedly deep-seated – fear of making images. Doesn't
the Second Commandment clearly state that we shall not
make graven images of what is above in heaven nor what
is below on earth nor what is in the waters below the
earth? So is it alright to just take a snap of an angel? Here
I come to her rescue. She only noticed later that there
was an angel in the picture: it appeared when the film
was developed. If it really was an angel, I think that it is
one of those examples which shows that they have a
sublime sense of humour in heaven; this photo could be
an example of Our Lord winking at us.

19 Photographs can produce some strange results. I have another photo taken by a woman of the horizon in the East just before the sun rose on 25 December 1989. You can see the line of the horizon shining, the sharply silhouetted outlines of poplars and in the distance a small church tower.

Above the church tower the figure of an angel is clearly visible. The woman who took the photo did not notice it until afterwards.

Is this a photograph of a real angel? Is it possible that the members of the congregation were told something about angels during the early morning church service and that their thoughts were projected into the sky?

This is not really as crazy as it sounds. De la Warr took a photograph of ordinary water and holy water with his strange "black box". His camera, which records a finer part of the material world on the photographic plate than the purely material world, revealed the distinct shape of a cross in the holy water. It turned out that the priest who blessed the water always thought of a cross during the blessing.

The world is much more complicated than we think, and our thoughts can have a strong influence on our environment. Thus I do not know why there is an angel in this photograph, but it is certainly impressive.

Unfortunately, we were not so lucky with the incident in the Russian space ship the Salyut 7. Vladimir Solivev, Oleg Atkov and Leonid Kizim allegedly saw "seven gigantic figures with a human appearance and wings as large as jumbo jets surrounded by a hazy aura" on the 155th day of their long space flight. According to American press reviews reported in *Paranormal* (June 1986): "They had round faces and smiled angelically."

What can you say about this? In my view this is clearly a "monkey roll". Surely these thoroughly trained astronauts would have taken a photograph straightaway. Perhaps the flight leaders would not allow them to, because angels do not exist and so you cannot photograph them. No, I think this story has a definite "monkey roll" feeling. In fact, this story is also told in different words.

I have an American newspaper report lying in front of me. There is a large headline:

"Space telescope photographs angels".

The report is given below:

"Scientists have been given an astonishing proof that heaven exists because the spectacular Hubble space telescope has sent images to earth of real live angels. Prominent astronauts say that the photographs of angels composed by the computer have not been publicly distributed because of the fear of worldwide panic. But sources that have inspected the photographs say that they are the most important data which have ever been collected."

According to NASA sources, the angels were a bright orange colour. At first, scientists thought that they had discovered a new star cluster because the colours were so bright and strong. But a few minutes later it was clear that they were looking at lifesize figures. According to a secret report a group of seven angels were flying together on photographs taken of the three billion year old star cluster NGC 3532.

Is this a monkey roll story? I have no doubt that it is.

The report also states that the angels had "round and peaceful faces, wings as wide as an airplane, and that they were surrounded by an aura". Obviously this is the same story as that told by the Russian astronauts, but told in different words. So this was a fake report, but why? The strange thing about this story is that it is told at all. Even though it falls into the "angel on the motorway" category, why does the human mind conjure up these stories?

The first Russian astronaut said that he had been to heaven but had not met God there. Are the space angels a sort of good-natured revenge for that remark? Wouldn't it be fun if it were true and the three astronauts would have been able to say to the first spaceman on their return: "No, we didn't see God, but we did see some angels."

An angel photographed from an airplane, seven enormous angels seen from a space ship and photographed with the Hubble telescope – what are we thinking of? We have even managed to incorporate heaven in our materialist view of the world.

The mystery requires "scientific proof" to be recorded on the photosensitive plates, and the angels are described as having "wings like jumbo jets".

The world of the past, when there were elves, has been

transformed into a mechanical fairytale in which the horses of the elves are replaced by "flying saucers". The elves themselves are "UFOnauts" and are given wonderful names, which indicate that they have come to us from distant galaxies, instead of simply being called Oberon or Puck.

Sometimes I am horrified by our age in which the feeling for mystery has been lost, and everything that smacks of the mysterious is immediately crystalised into a technical concept. That is why I am relieved to leave these partly humourous and partly tragic stories behind me, and will go on to tell you about an experience of a woman who was about forty years old when she wrote to me.

20 Until she was 35, she led a life in which all her activities were based on materialistic considerations. She was seriously affected by a virus that made many people spiritually sick in the 1970s. This virus was called the "God is dead theory". Yet she seemed to be someone who was ready to move on from her caterpillar stage to her butterfly stage, and there was a great deal of sadness in her life. Gradually her rock-hard attitude wore away and during the famous "mid-life crisis" she found God in her life again. When this happened she remembered something that she had lost when she was seven years old.

The memory went back to when she was three years old. Some people think this is strange, but it is quite possible that there are people who remember things that young. She said that she was lying in bed asleep but suddenly woke up because her name was called out twice.

This is a typical Biblical phenomenon.

When Abraham had to sacrifice his son Isaac and the boy was tied up ready to be sacrificed, the angel of the Lord called to him from heaven and said: "Abraham, Abraham!" (Genesis 22:11).

When Samuel was called by God he heard: "Samuel, Samuel." (1 Samuel 3:10).

This double call is characteristic of a true story. The woman then wrote that there was a man standing next to her bed. She did not know whether he was young or middle-aged. His face was smooth but not young. His hair was curly but grey. He was dressed in a light grey

garment with wide sleeves and a material she subsequently identified as being linen. He was standing to
the right of her bed but he did not look at her. She
followed the direction of his gaze and immediately found
herself *in* a starry heaven. There was a silver cord, about
as thick as the tightrope on which circus performers walk,
going diagonally upwards from the right. The man put
her on his shoulders and walked up along the rope, but
she did not know where it ended.

This is the report I heard.

The story confirms certain indications that at night man
leaves his body and is carried to other spheres by angels.
The silver cord is mentioned in the Bible (Ecclesiastes,
12:6), which states that the cord is loosened upon death.
Just as the umbilical cord joins us to our mother's body,
this silver cord joins our mortal self, our body, to our
immortal self, our soul.

This little girl saw something which happens to every
child at night. I doubt whether it also happens to every
adult. I do not believe everyone is carried up at night.
Your destination depends on your daytime life.

Moreover, it is striking that when she was in the starry
heavens, the path along the cord led upwards. This is
significant and it is a response to the unreal angels of the
astronaut.

The starry sky that we see belongs to the material universe, and therefore it should still be included as part of
the "earth" in the sense of Genesis ("In the beginning
God created the heaven and the earth"). God's heaven
only starts beyond the starry sky. I do not mean it is
further away than the starry sky in the sense of a hundred
billion light years rather than a billion light years. I mean
this in the sense of it being "totally different". The first
Russian astronaut was right when he said he did not see
God anywhere. He was in the wrong inner space.
Although he was floating above the earth in space, he
was actually still on "earth", and would also have been
so if he had flown to a star in the Swan galaxy.

To make this woman's letter more readable, I have
changed it slightly. In fact, she describes the things that
I wrote down consecutively, as though they were scenes
which all took place at the same time. Just as the man
next to her bed was timeless, the experience itself was

also timeless. The double call of her name was reflected in the oneness of the past and the future, in a timeless NOW.

This sort of story has a good feeling about it. It has a better feeling than any photograph of angels ever taken, simply because it is less tangible and more subjective. There is more mystery contained in it, as there should be in any experience of angels.

It is interesting to take a closer look at this woman's life, as she described it.

It can clearly be divided into three stages.

1. From the age of three to seven she was a child with deep religious feeling. She was also a child with great inner strength.
2. This was followed by a period of chaos and lost feeling which lasted from the age of seven to 35 (the so-called 'mid-point' of life) when the great central memory which had pervaded her early youth – of the angel taking her with him – completely disappeared.
3. After a transitional phase of suffering she felt an almost mystical oneness with God. But while her childhood link was unconscious, she had now become conscious, purified by fire as it were, and every day she was faced with new choices.

The woman finished her letter with the words: "Does an oyster enjoy its own pearl? It is the sun which makes it shine." This is a beautiful ending. Pearls are created from the oyster's pain. They are the valuable tears of the sea. Suffering is meaningful if man learns to answer this, not with the question "why" uttered in despair, but with the word "wherefore", uttered with faith. This is actually the correct translation of Jesus's words on the Cross: "My God, my God where*fore* hast thou forsaken me?" The word "why" looks back, the word "wherefore" leads to the future and can even give meaning to the most severe suffering.

The question arises: Wherefore did this great experience happen *first*, to be followed by a period of being lost?

The Jews answer this question in a singular way. They argue that if there were no exile, man could never experience the joy of coming home.

Coming home brings such joy that the preceding exile makes it worthwhile.

If you look at this story carefully, it is as though God first secured this woman like a mountaineer is tied, and then let her undertake the climb knowing that if she fell, the fall might be very great, but not so great that she would be smashed to pieces.

Psalm 145:14 reads: 'The Lord upholdesth all that fall.'

My Hebrew teacher pointed out that the Hebrew words actually state: 'He upholdeth, the Lord, all that fall.'

In other words, first He secures the supports very strongly just as a mountaineer hammers his pitons into the rock, and then he starts climbing so that if he falls, the lifeline is absolutely secure.

It is precisely because there was a period of darkness after her experience of the angel and before the light broke through, that this woman's story can be included as one of the true stories of angels. If the angel had smiled sweetly, as for the astronauts, and she had lived happily ever after, I would not have marked her letter with the red words "true angels".

CHAPTER 3

ANGELS IN AND
AROUND OUR
HOUSE

The following chapter deals with a number of different matters. We spend a significant part of our time in and around the house. We are born there, we sleep there, we grow up there. We eat our meals there and enjoy our free time. We experience joy and love there, and also have times of sickness and despair. Finally, we die there – at least if we are lucky enough to escape death in hospital.

Therefore the word 'home' has a very special feeling which does not compare with anything else. It is by no means a coincidence that going to heaven is often compared with 'coming home'. So it is not surprising that many experiences with angels take place in and around the home. Angels like to be in a good home. 'Be not forgetful to entertain strangers: for thereby some have entertained angels unawares.' (Hebrews 13:2).

I will start with a few examples of angels which simply appear. You get the feeling that they enjoy the house where they are and therefore appear for a minute.

Angels Which 'Simply' Appear

21 Imagine a beautiful summer's day. This story took place just before sunrise. A woman was sleeping in her bedroom, which had a window facing east. Suddenly she woke up because there was a sound like an eggshell breaking, and immediately she felt that there was someone there. She opened her eyes and on the windowsill she saw a human figure, his knees drawn up, dressed in a long garment which covered his feet. She saw this figure silhouetted darkly against the eastern sky which was rapidly getting lighter. He had two wings which were white, contrasting with the background. The strange thing was that there were several white strings hanging down from the wings. He even touched one string and she heard a note.

Immediately she was filled with an indescribable sense of joy. This joy did not remain constant but quickly increased and became almost intolerable. She compared it with the pain which can also cross the border of what is tolerable, and become intolerable. She had the feeling that if her joy increased any further, there was a danger that she would burst and she said to herself: 'No!' The joy filled every corner of her being and overpowered her so totally that she literally had to hold onto her existence with her hands and feet.

She didn't know whether this situation lasted a second or half an hour, but with the first ray of sunshine everything disappeared even more quickly than if something was erased.

This experience had a strange sequel, for a few days later her husband said to her in surprise: 'Why are you walking round with that loving look on your face, what's the matter with you?'

She could not answer. After all she could hardly say to him that she had fallen in love with an angel. He would have called the doctor straight away. She had never told this story to anyone else until she read my book about angels and decided to write to me. Angels are often depicted with harps, but in this case it is as though the angel himself was a musical instrument. The broken eggshell is very significant. All of Creation has sometimes been compared to an egg. Inside this shell is everything we perceive with our senses, from the smallest ant to the immense galaxies. The shell is the boundary which God made at the beginning of Creation. It is because of this boundary that we are able to develop in freedom.

Outside this egg is the other world, God's heaven and its inhabitants. As I said before, this is no further away than the galaxies, but is divided from us by an invisible wall. Did the angel in this story come 'by chance'? The experience was preceded by a very strange incident. Two years before, the woman had been in Rome. When she visited a church she happened to be standing next to a group of people from India. While the guide was explaining something, a little boy of about six years old gestured to her. When she bent down he placed both his hands on her forehead and said something while he looked at her with a very grave expression. She asked his father what he was saying and he answered in English: 'He is praying for your happiness'. Upon her surprised request why he should do that for her, the father did not answer, but turned to his wife and said something to her in his own language. The child's mother bowed down deeply in front of her. Then the father picked up the child and went away, but as long as the boy could see her he held his hands stretched out towards her in a blessing.

She herself made a connection between the little boy praying for her happiness and the experience of the angel which took place two years later. It was very good to be blessed by a child. 'For I say unto you, that in heaven the angels do always behold the face of my Father which is in heaven.' (Matthew 18:10).

A significant aspect of this woman's letter was that she described in detail the consequences of her experiences with angels on the rest of her life. 'From that time my life was torn in two.' She hates having people round or visiting people because she cannot tolerate small talk. She feels that most of her contact with other people is empty and her spiritual ear seems to hear 'things behind things'. She also said: 'When I listen to people chatting, it seems to me that there is more point in a flock of sparrows quarreling in a bush.' For anyone who experiences the eggshell breaking, life is never the same again. It would be very interesting to hear from other people what are

the effects wrought in them by their experience of an
angel. This is not related to the experience of the angel
itself, but what actually happens in the human soul. At
the end of this book I will make an attempt to evaluate
these effects. For several reasons the following incident
is also worth recounting.

22 One morning a middle-aged woman woke up
earlier than usual and found to her great surprise
that an angel was floating above her bed. She was so
surprised that she called out several times: 'An angel, a
real angel, my guardian angel!' Then she gave a very
precise description of this apparition. He was between
1.7 and 1.8 m tall and had fair hair which did not fall
over his face, even though he was floating horizontally.
He was wearing a long white garment which covered his
feet and which was not sharply outlined, but rather like
a cloud which does not have a clear edge. He was wearing
a beautiful bright blue belt about 20 cm wide and his
arms were crossed over his chest. When she tried to look
at his face he turned his head away slightly. After about
ten minutes he made a small movement with his elbows
and disappeared again, but a wonderful smell of roses
remained behind in the bedroom and stayed there for
several hours. The woman was filled with a deep sense of
happiness. In this story several things deserve particular
attention.
– The angel's feet were covered.
This is characteristic of many stories about angels. In
Isaiah 6:2 the seraphim's feet were covered.
– The remark the woman made about the angel floating
horizontally although his hair did not fall over his face.
In the dimension where angels live, the laws of gravity
do not apply.
– The sky-blue belt: Exodus 28 describes the clothes of
a priest. The ordinary priest wore a completely white
garment but his belt was made of wool of three colours
and one of those colours was sky-blue.
Therefore the angel was dressed almost like an ordinary
priest from the Old Testament. A High Priest was
dressed differently. For example, he wore a sky-blue
cloak bordered with golden bells and pomegranates. Perhaps the garments of this woman's angel indicated it was

an 'ordinary' angel, the lowest on the ladder of the nine hierarchies.

– Finally, the smell of roses which remained behind is very characteristic. This phenomenon occurs several times after experiences of angels.

23 The third story is by a woman who was weeding her garden two weeks before she wrote to me. The date was 29 August 1988. It was half past four in the afternoon and the sun was shining brightly. Suddenly she had the feeling that there was someone standing behind her. She looked around and saw someone standing about one metre away. She was immediately completely overwhelmed by this apparition's penetrating gaze. He was dressed in a shining white garment and he was very tall. She does not know how long this lasted, but suddenly he was gone. However, for a long time she could see his wonderful eyes wherever she looked.

This is another characteristic phenomenon which indicates this was a true angel. One of my colleagues had a similar experience walking through a snowy landscape and all he said about it was: 'That gaze . . . that gaze'.

24 A woman of 88 wrote me the following story. During the night of the 2nd to the 3rd of January 1989 she was sleeping quietly when she suddenly woke up. She looked up in surprise, turned her head to the right towards the bathroom and saw a young man aged about 25 standing there. He was no further than one metre from her bed standing in her walking frame. He had a strikingly beautiful face and was dressed in light blue clothes. His hair was dark and short. He did not say anything, but made a reassuring gesture with his hand. A beautiful shining bright light filled the room. (She added that it was not like her own yellow light.) This light radiated great peace. It lasted about three or four minutes, and then the light and the young man suddenly disappeared. She was certainly wide awake and was not dreaming. In these days when the virtues of youth are constantly extolled, we often tend not to take old people seriously – unlike the more civilized people of past centuries. An old lady like that all alone at night – just imagine!

That is why I would like to conclude this story with a very moving confirmation that it was true. The Sunday after this experience she had her eighty-eighth birthday and her eldest daughter gave her a book. It was a Moravian diary with a suitable text for every day of the year. When her daughter had gone she opened the page for the 3rd of January and saw: 'The Lord will send his angel with you and will put you on the path of prosperity.' With great simplicity she wondered what this meant for she was only an ordinary person. The effect of this experience on her life is that since that time she has had a wonderful feeling of happiness and her faith has been strengthened. Despite her rather stiff right hand, she managed to laboriously write this story down for me and I am grateful to her. She may be an ordinary person, but when she wrote down this story, she was no longer ordinary. At the end of her life the butterfly started to crawl out of its cocoon. In heaven there are no ordinary people, only special people, just as every child is unique and special in the eyes of its parents, even if they have a number of children.

The Biblical text which applies so aptly to the event of the 3rd of January obviously does not count as proof for a skeptic. Many people will think that it proves nothing. We should remember that there are two sorts of proof. One is scientific proof which is based on experiment, repeating the experience and statistical probability.

However, there is also another sort of proof. This is based on what we normally call coincidence. Two people meet at exactly the right moment. By 'coincidence' someone just misses a plane which crashes. A strange dream provides the solution to a problem. These things prove that there is a guiding thread in our lives and that God has not lost control. However, this sort of proof is only valid for those who have eyes to see it.

Moreover, life is not a bed of roses. In the days before the entertainment industry took over, it was often called a vale of tears and behind the glittering facade of the myriad television shows, it remains a vale of tears. That is why the next section deals with:

ANGELS AS COMFORTERS

One of the names of The Holy Ghost is the Comforter.
Angels are often concerned with consolation. In 1968, the
following incident took place:

▷ **25** Just imagine a cold drizzly night in November. In
the distance the church tower struck midnight and
a woman who had been working that evening in a large
hotel walked home through the dark streets of a town in
the Netherlands.

On her way she passed a pub and saw her husband's
moped. She looked in through the window and saw her
husband standing there, rather tipsy, feeling up a rather
brash young woman. She exploded with rage, stormed
into the pub, kicked her husband and the other woman
hard on the shins, and then ran out.

This sounds rather like a tragi-comedy but that is because
we are reading the story from the outside. If you remember that this was the mother of a family, who had been
working hard all day, and then found her husband in
this state, the story looks quite different. It is easy to
understand that she felt more and more miserable as she
walked through the dark city in the drizzle. She
remembered that she had only had harsh words from her
husband and that he had turned her sons against her.

She thought that her life was no longer worth living.
Halfway across a deserted bridge over a canal she stood
still and stared sadly into the black water below her. She
bade farewell to everything and saw her whole life pass
by in front of her, but just before she decided to jump,
she suddenly saw a man standing there. He was a striking
figure 1.8 m tall with broad shoulders and curly white
hair. She could not see his face well because it was hidden
in the shadows. He was dressed like a priest and wore a
cross on his lapel. The man started to talk to her but she
said: 'Oh, just go away or I'll start to scream.' However,
he did not consider going away, and went on talking to
her. He asked her whether she had children and she
started to talk to him about her sons and tell him their
names. Then he said something very strange: 'I know all
about your misery but remember that above all, you are
a mother. No mother has the right to deliberately leave

her children without a mother.' For the first time she tried to look him straight in the eyes but his face was still in the shadows. However, she could see that he was smiling in a friendly way and when he said: 'Come on, I will walk a little way with you to the light.'

Slowly they walked down the bridge and when they had gone a little way they arrived at the station. 'Right', he said, 'now you are in the light', and he indicated that he was going to leave. 'Can you tell me your name?' she asked. 'Because I would like to write to you.' He merely laughed and said: 'What's in a name?' Then he said goodbye.

She had to turn right and he turned left on the deserted station square. After two steps she turned round, but the man had vanished without trace. It was as though he had been dissolved in the air. The woman's marriage was troubled but she felt a deep sense that God is Love. I do not know whether you have noticed, but there is an interesting Biblical parallel to this story.

Judges 13 is about a man called Manoah whose wife was infertile. Then an angel of the Lord appeared to her and announced the birth of a very special son who would liberate Israel from the dominion of the Philistines. Later he would be the judge, Samson. Manoah also met the angel and he asked: 'What is thy name, that when thy sayings come to pass we may do thee honour?' (Judges 13:17).

The angel answered: 'Why askest thou thus after my name, seeing it is secret?' God's angels have names usually ending in 'el', but these examples show that they sometimes keep their names secret. Is this how they prevent the honour which their King deserves from going to them?

Someone might say: 'Why did that angel on the bridge look like a Roman Catholic priest?' The explanation seems obvious. Just as an angel often appears as a child so as not to frighten the little one, this angel appeared to the devout Catholic woman as an elderly priest. The purpose of the encounter was consolation and for this he first had to make her feel at ease. To achieve this, God dresses his servants in appropriate garments for He is extremely careful with his children.

As we have seen before there are certain patterns in stories about angels. The story recounted above is by no means unique.

26 A married woman, a mother of three children, was overcome by a feeling of utter despair. These days depression is all too common, even though we live in such a prosperous material age. But people often have a sense of meaninglessness. One evening the woman got into a train to Rotterdam wearing her slippers. When she arrived, she walked out to the harbour feeling utterly depressed, and stood looking out over the River Maas for a while. She felt the urge to swim to the other side and in this way play a sort of Russian roulette.

She decided that if she arrived she would survive, but if she drowned, that was fine with her. Suddenly, there was a young man next to her on the deserted quayside, though she had not seen him arrive. He put his arm through hers and said: 'We certainly won't do that. Come on, we're going to have a cup of coffee.'

Nearby, there was a depot for containers and next to the depot there was a coffee-bar which was still open. They drank two cups of coffee and the man said to her: 'You live in The Hague, and now you're going home Brigitte, because you can manage that.'

How did the man know all this? She had not told him her name, nor where she lived. She said goodbye to him and went back home.

Later she returned to that spot which was engraved on her memory. The strange thing was that there was no coffee-bar to be seen anywhere. She asked the dock workers what had happened to the coffee bar. But they looked at her as though she was mad and said that there had never been one.

Can a visitor from Heaven conjure up a complete coffee-bar so that he can sit and drink a cup of coffee with the person he is protecting?

Why shouldn't this be possible? Everything we see was created because the Creator expressed his thoughts. God merely has to think of a coffee-bar and there it is, and when he stops thinking about the coffee-bar it disappears as though it had never been.

Creation is much more flexible than we are, for we try to tie everything down, in our thoughts. God not only created the world in the past but He is constantly creating new things.

I hope I am not treading on anyone's toes when I say this, but I am supported by no less a person than the prophet Isaiah who says: 'I have showed thee new things from this time, even hidden things, and thou didst not know them. They are created now, and not from the beginning; even before the day when thou heardest them not.' (Isaiah 48:6).

God does not live in a succession of events but in an eternal now, in which His six creative stages as well as His day of rest are eternally present. It is only for us that moments succeed each other in time.

Thus, the two stories above show that in addition to serving as messengers and rescuers, angels also console us. And we do not have to go far to find a Biblical parallel. In Genesis 21, Hagar, Abraham's second wife, and Ishmael, her son, the patriarch of all the Arabs, are in danger of perishing from thirst when they have been banished into the desert

Hagar moved her son a little way away because she could no longer endure the sight of his suffering. She wept and Ishmael wept too. Then an angel appeared from heaven and talked to her with compassion: 'What is the matter? Do not be afraid!' At first the angel consoled her, only later did he give her instructions and show her a well.

The following story is a wonderful story about consolation:

27 A woman had lost her mother when she was only a year-and-a-half old. Some people think that this may not have much effect as long as a good replacement mother is found. You don't really remember the second year of your life.

However, this is not the case.

I have come across people who suddenly went into deep mourning and this could be traced back to the loss of one or both parents during the second year of their life. Thus they have been orphaned at an age which usually doesn't fall within our memory.

The woman I am describing here grew up with an enormous sense of nostalgia in her heart, and because this sorrow had arisen before the time that she could talk, she was unable to express her sorrow. The nostalgia not only continued to overshadow her whole life, but it constantly increased because there was nothing to oppose its growth. Only sorrow which has been consciously experienced has a chance of being integrated.

When she was 20 years old she was sitting in a church with beautiful stained glass windows on Christmas Day, and as so often in her life she was overcome by a profound sense of nostalgia. It even seemed more intense than usual.

Then something wonderful happened. A great angel with spread-out wings came gliding towards her through one of the stained glass windows. The angel had the face of her mother as she recognized it from photographs. This was followed by something the young woman was unable to describe because she cannot find any words to express it. It was as though her whole being was embraced with a caressing feeling. It was as though she was in Heaven. Then the angel disappeared but from that time she never had the feeling of nostalgia again. One of the most moving passages in her letter is when she writes: 'I have a rather down-to-earth nature. This really happened!'

In this way she placed the event in the middle of her daily life and made it just as real as a meeting with a loved one. I will not speculate whether her mother had become an angel or whether the angel had assumed the face of her mother. Everyone can decide this for themselves.

The main thing is that her life was made whole at a stroke. The consolation which comes from Heaven is so important that I would like to give some more examples of it. I hope that it will give strength to many unhappy people. Let them remember that even if you do not see any angels, consolation is always pouring down upon us.

28 In 1952 there was a young woman aged 22 at a Bible school in the district of Hessen in Germany. She wanted to train to help in her church at home. Like everywhere in Europe at that time – and even now – this school had also been affected by the 'scientific attitude'. This is one of the best ways which has been devised to help young people to lose their faith. Many questions were approached with the help of the books

of Bultmann. Towards Whitsun everyone went home
but the woman, who lived in Lower Saxony, had no
money for the trip.

Her father had died in the war and her mother had fled
to the West with her – the eldest daughter – and her six
sisters, to escape the advancing Russian army. Thus, her
family was poverty-stricken and she remained behind in
the empty Bible school quite alone. She felt extremely
abandoned and unhappy. On the Saturday before Whitsun her unhappy mood deepened to utter despair. She
was overcome with great doubt that she would be able
to fulfill her role of helping with the work for the church.
Admittedly she found studying easy enough, but she had
a very clear feeling that the essential element could not
be found in her books. She had become so confused that
she no longer really knew what Whitsun meant. With a
shock she realised how helpless she would be if children
or young people asked her for the meaning of Whitsun.
That evening she prayed fervently for some insight into
the meaning of Whitsun. She hoped that on Whit Sunday
she might hear a sermon in the church which would give
her the answer. She awoke very early on the morning of
Whit Sunday. At the foot of her bed on the left she saw
a great shining angel. He looked as though he was made
entirely of transparent gold. He stood very still with his
gaze turned inward and radiated both deep peace and an
indescribable exaltation. The walls of the bedroom and
the ceiling were no obstacle for him. His head and his
back reached through the walls.

She was so frightened that she shut her eyes tight and
then carefully peeped through her eyelashes but the angel
was still standing there. She pulled the covers over her
head and thought: 'I'm losing my mind'. Then she took
another cautious look over the edge of the covers and
saw that he was starting to fade away and become hazy
as though a light was being slowly extinguished.

She felt as though everything had been jumbled up inside
her and she tried to convince herself that it had all been
an illusion, but her heart clearly told her that an illusion
would not have had such a profound effect.

She never dared to breathe a word about this experience
to anyone from the Bible school, because she felt sure it
would have been attributed to religious stress and that in

this era of Bultmann's ideas no one would take angels seriously. It was more than twenty years before she was able to talk to anyone about it. I think that this story of a young woman hiding under the blankets in fright is so understandable and so moving, that I certainly could not have left it out.

There are two aspects to which I would like to draw attention:

1. The prayer for an insight into the meaning of Whitsun, which was heard in such a way that she was not given any teachings, but an experience which caused total inner confusion.

2. The struggle which took place between her head (you're crazy) and the heart (this is real); fortunately the heart won. "Now my eye has perceived you . . ."

The appearance of the angel was the explanation of Whitsun, viz., the appearance of Heaven on our dark earth.

We know that angels can play a role in prayer which is a struggle. The great example of this in Christianity can be found in Gethsemene, when Jesus was on the point of being taken prisoner. In great distress, he prayed:

"Father if thou be willing, remove this cup from me: nevertheless, not my will, but thine be done. And there appeared an angel unto him from heaven strengthening him." (Luke 22: 42,43). The next story also took place in Germany.

29 The woman who told this story was 37 years old at the time. In 1962, after waiting for a long time, she was to move into a home of her own with her husband and four children, for the first time in her married life. The family was extremely happy, but soon afterwards her husband fell ill. Then came the terrible day that the doctor told her that her husband was suffering from a disease from which he would not recover. She sank into deep despair.

That night, when everyone was asleep, she got up and knelt down and started to pray fervently for her husband's life.

"No, no!" she called softly. "Why should this happen? Oh Father in Heaven, don't let this happen . . ."

The longer she prayed the more she realised that she would have to accept God's will without any reservations, even if it was decided that her husband would die. This insight made her even sadder and she sat down at the table in deep distress, her head bowed down, her hands in front of her face, and completely filled with fear. To accept the loss of her husband? Was that what was meant?

She struggled with the idea and could not accept it. She simply did not have it in her.

In the darkest night, she sat utterly alone.

Then she looked up and saw a light figure standing in front of her. She thought it was Jesus. The figure reached out his hand to her and said: "Have faith".

When she found the courage to take hold of the hand, the room was filled with an indescribably bright light, despite the fact that the light was on. It completely surrounded her and gave her the strength to consciously accept whatever happened with a great sense of inner joy.

"Yes, Your Will be done," she said with utter conviction. She was indescribably relieved. By now the night had come to an end and with a sense of cheerful acceptance she started to lay the breakfast table festively as though it was Christmas morning. She was so different that her husband asked her in the morning what was the matter. She found it impossible to talk about the events and therefore she said something different:

"You know that you have to go to hospital today and your mother is coming to be close to us. I'd like everything to be cheerful for her so that she's not sad that you're in hospital".

This was not a white lie. One of the things which she had struggled with in her prayers in the night was the question of how she would tell her mother-in-law that there was no hope for her son. She now knew that she would have to do this, not in a spirit of mourning, but in a mood of solemn joy. Joy about dying? When a good person dies, it is as if they are promoted. We cannot see that from here, but this woman had understood it in her experience that night. There is a sort of heavenly economy which determines that we receive what we give to others.

30) One clear example of that principle in which the gentle insistence of an angel also played a role, is the following story. A much loved member of my family

had a serious accident in a city abroad. In his own world he is an important and much respected man, but in that city he was picked up from the street, an unknown person, and was taken to an over-crowded dirty hospital ward with poor care. He was in a great deal of pain, he was lonely, and he gradually became desperate because he did not know what would happen.

Then he turned to God with a serious prayer.

After saying this prayer he was lying staring into space and unexpectedly his arm was taken and he was gently guided to the man lying next to him who was terribly ill. This man was in an even worse state than he was himself. Although he could not see anyone guiding his arm and his hand, he heard a voice saying that he must touch his neighbour and hold him and in this way he consoled the poor man, forgetting his own sorrow. By helping the other man, they were helped together.

This same principle of Heavenly economy also operates in people who faithfully give a tenth of their income (in all sorts of ways in practice) and realize that they always have enough left for their own needs.

I once came across an American evangelist who turned this principle round and said something like this: "If you want more money, then give me a tenth of your income. It will be as if you have sown your money, and you will reap a good harvest". This is doing good in order to benefit yourself, and anyone who does this is folding his butterfly wings and metamorphosing back into a caterpillar. It sounds frightening, but it certainly is possible. However, it is definitely not the best way.

ANGELS AND HEALING

Salvation, consolation, messages, strength for hard times – these are all activities related to angels. Very often they take place in secret: in the living room, the bedroom, the garden, and even the people around have noticed nothing.

The aspects of meetings with angels which I will describe now is related to healing. I do this with due modesty because there is a vast literature about people who are healed by God's touch. For example, the books of Kathryn Kuhlmann spring to mind. A healing experience by the Holy Ghost is one of the greatest miracles in medicine. I would like to focus on just one sort of such Heavenly cures, viz., those cases in which angels were clearly involved. I hope I am expressing myself clearly: a cure in which an angel is seen or involved, is always a cure by the Holy Ghost. The angel is a manifestation of God's power to heal the sick if that is part of the plan of Creation. This healing can also take place directly without any angels being seen. Prayers for healing are not always heard, as we saw in the story about the woman who moved into her new house just before her husband became incurably ill. This is a bitter experience for anyone who prays and in many cases it is incomprehensible. I will give a number of examples here, in which people were miraculously cured. The first case is doubly significant. Not only does it concern a healing, but we also come across a particular pattern which is fairly common in encounters with angels. I would like to call this phenomenon "the angel in the doorway".

31 The story I am about to tell took place in 1970. It is about a woman who was in her early forties, the mother of three children. She started the change of life too early and felt absolutely terrible. She was physically ill, but the worst thing was her deep depression. She really wanted her life to be over, but she had three children, and thinking about them stopped her taking her life. One night as she lay awake, her wish to die was so strong that she hoped that she would die that very night. Then suddenly and quite unexpectedly she was filled with an enormous will to go on living after all. She prayed fervently to be restored to health. She was lying in the dark praying with her whole heart and soul. Then the door of her room opened about one third of the way, and in the doorway there was an enormous shining figure. His head touched the top of the door. As she looked at this figure in total amazement, her soul was filled with a profound sense of tranquillity and indescribable peace. She did not know how long this lasted but when it was over she fell asleep. The next morning she had the feeling that her life had been completely changed and in a few weeks she was restored to physical and

spiritual health. Since that time she has never felt the wish
to die.

32 In order to give the reader a good impression of
this sort of experience I will give another example.
This is about a German woman, twenty-seven-years-old
and a mother of two children. The incident took place in
1960.

She had been suffering from deep depression for some
time. The letter does not indicate if this was post-natal
depression but the symptoms suggest that this was the
case. Most people have heard of this serious affliction
which can affect women when they have just given birth,
and which in serious cases can constitute a danger for
both the mother and the child. Sometimes this condition
only starts a few weeks after the birth, but it can also
start immediately. For example, one of my colleagues
saw this condition start as he was tying the baby's umbilical cord. The woman who had given birth suddenly
became so confused and wild that she knocked his glasses
from his nose.

The German woman I mentioned felt – in her own words
– "completely turned to stone". She felt a deadly inner
loneliness and complete isolation which is only felt by
patients suffering from deep depression.

At the time when this incident took place, her husband
was in hospital waiting for an operation. One day when
she visited him and opened the door to his room there
was an enormous angel in front of her, just in the opening
of the door. He looked at her with indescribable intensity
and piercing eyes. He radiated such an overwhelming
force that she had the feeling of a heavy weight being
pressed down on her so that she was almost forced to
kneel down. However, she rejected that feeling and stood
her ground. Then the apparition dissolved and she saw
her husband lying in bed with the anaesthetist sitting next
to him, discussing his operation. She was very confused
and frightened and noticed straightaway that the others
had not seen anything. For many weeks she was almost
unable to talk as a result of this incident and subsequently
she kept silent about it for twenty-four years.

Before saying something else about her, I would like to
note that depressions such as hers are not accompanied

by hallucinations. The woman was not cured instantaneously but the confrontation with the angel was a turning point and she clearly saw that this incident was part of the healing process of her long-lasting depression.

Once again there is a strange interconnection between a meeting with angels and the path followed by a person in his life. The "Versteinerung" (which I translated as being turned to stone) which this woman mentioned – actually a better description than our own term "depression" – may have been the stage at which her soul underwent a metamorphosis. The encounter with the angel then represents the moment at which the cocoon starts to burst open and the butterfly is on the point of emerging. The tremendous radiation of the angel burst her cocoon.

In the next few months she gradually appeared with the moist and clumsy, but true wings of her soul.

It is worth noting that the angel didn't "do" anything. He just stood there and looked. He was like the Zen master who gave a tap at just the right moment so that the stone prison broke. These are only two of the many examples I could cite in which an angel is seen through a half-open door. The real door of the (bed)room then serves as a symbol for the mysterious door to another world about which St. John writes in the Book of Revelations:

"After this I looked, and behold, a door was opened in the heaven." (Revelations 4:1).

Between this world and the more spiritual world there are holes in the net. A lively exchange takes place through these holes. Usually we don't notice this but from time to time it suddenly becomes visible and we are overwhelmed by the beauty and majesty which lies beyond the threshold.

33 A third example of an astonishing cure is that of a woman who had been plagued for many years by the most terrible nightmares. Anyone who has ever suffered from these knows how bad it can be. The paralysing fear, the impossibility of escape, the cold sweat, the palpitations . . . Many people who experienced terrible things in the war never managed to lose these nightmares.

One night this woman woke up. She looked round the

room and saw someone standing on the left-hand side of her bed. She was frightened and woke up her husband but he could not see anything. Although the room was dark she could see very well. She described this apparition as follows:

He was very tall, very beautiful and above all she was struck by his beautifully formed hands. He was dressed in a purple cloak with an orange, violet and purple sash across his chest. He was wearing something strange on his head, a triangular, indigo headdress and he radiated an alert sense of peace.

Then he began to talk to her without using words. She simply knew what he was saying, which she found very strange. He told her that he was guarding over her and that she need never be afraid again, because the demons would never return.

Then he said: "Now go to sleep," and immediately she fell asleep, just like a small child can suddenly fall asleep. She wrote to me about five years after this had happened, but she had never had nightmares again.

There are several striking things in this letter which require further explanation.

In the first place, there is the fact that she consistently placed the word "nightmares" in quotation marks. It is as though she wanted to indicate in this way that there was more to it.

I have heard people talk of nightmares like complaints several times in my capacity as a doctor. Upon closer consideration they occasionally turned out to be something else.

I am thinking of people in my practice who had been members of the resistance. They had to liquidate people in the war and were later attacked by their victims at night.

I am thinking of a girl with a spiritualist background who was sexually abused by a black man at night. Admittedly this was like a nightmare, but when a friend went to watch over her at night she heard footsteps coming up the stairs. The door of the room opened very slowly even though there was no one in the house except the girl and the friend watching over her.

I have mentioned only these cases, but there are several corresponding ones. These are not concerned with true nightmares but with forms of being possessed. With these people the door to the underworld sometimes swings open for some reason and demons slip through it. Not only do angels exist; unfortunately demons exist as well. The angel who cured this woman of her "nightmares" therefore made the right diagnosis. He did not waste time by talking about nightmares but stated in a very matter of fact way that they were demons and then he sealed the door to the underworld.

I do not know why the trapdoor to the underworld was ajar in this woman. Spiritualism may have caused the weak spot in her soul. But similarly a terrible shock such as a bomb attack or an unexpected severe fall, can tear the soul in this way.

The second fact I would like to analyze concerns the clothes this angel was wearing. I cannot elaborate on this here, but there is a reason why some angels are so splendidly dressed. In this day and age we find ceremonial dress rather ridiculous, even childish. Ours is an age of overalls, badly fitting suits, leisure wear and sports clothes. In fact, this does not say anything about the person wearing such clothes. "The apparel oft proclaims the man" is a well known saying – an inaccurate proverb. It would be more correct to say that clothes cover the man and often also conceal him.

However, in the regions of Heaven, every garment indicates a particular quality. F. Weinreb taught a whole course on this subject in which he explained that those things which are described in the Bible, such as the clothes of a priest, actually referred to qualities which the person concerned had in that life.

The sash with three colours which the above-mentioned angel was wearing is also one of the garments of priests, though in slightly different colours. Thus, because of the precise description of the colour of the angel's clothes, we can tell something of his character.

I will restrict myself here to the colours.

A purple cloak. Purple is violet and red.

An orange, purple and violet sash . . . violet, purple and orange.

An indigo headdress. Indigo is . . . a very intense blue.

When we add all these things together we see that there is a clear dominant colour blue, the blue end of the spectrum is dominant.

Blue is the colour of the Archangel Raphael, the angel whose name means: "God heals". Therefore, we know that because of this short analysis the angel belonged with Raphael, perhaps he was even Raphael.

In the above cases the mere presence of the angel was enough to help the patient become cured. The angel did almost nothing, he was simply there.

The following case was rather more complicated.

In my archives I have several letters from people who have had a number of encounters with angels in their lives. It seems that for them, the door to the other world is constantly ajar. These stories are well known in the history of mankind. For example, there are some Jewish stories which tell that Abraham was often visited by angels.

34 The woman in the next story told me about an incident which took place in 1983. She had an operation on her right kidney. During the operation she felt extremely anxious. Of course, it should not happen, but things sometimes go wrong under an anaesthetic. When she was feeling most anxious it was as though she was in a dark tunnel where she heard all sorts of horrible noises. At the end she could see a wonderful green light.

I would like to add that this was clearly an experience such as those of people who have almost died and which are often described in modern literature, for example, in the books by Moody.

When she arrived at the light she saw a human face. She merely said that it was a face with black hair. Then she heard a man's voice saying:

"Just listen to me. You are very sick, sicker than the doctors think. Remember what I am saying to you. Drink a lot of cold water every time you are in pain. Just remember, drink a lot. It will be two years before you're your old self again. You must learn from this experience for you should know what it means to be sick. Now go back through the tunnel. I am guarding over you. It is not time yet. Go, and do not be afraid."

She obeyed the voice immediately.

She went back through the tunnel, which was very easy this time, and heard the doctor call: "Thank God, she's made it. Give her more oxygen. This mustn't happen again."

Apparently, this patient had almost succumbed during the operation.

This incident had a very strange effect on her. Whenever she is unhappy she sees the reflection of two figures with wings high on their back in a window pane. Their faces are full of love, but she cannot see whether they are men or women. They have long hair and are standing in a bright light. They fill her with great joy so that she never feels alone or helpless and knows that she always has support.

There are two aspects of this story which I would particularly like to emphasize.

1. The woman was not cured immediately. This would have been possible, but it did not happen because there was something she had to learn. She was given some very good and simple advice which seems to come from natural medicine, viz., to drink lots of good water for her kidneys. This is pleasing for a doctor to hear because it is like a confirmation of his professional ideas. In the Bible there are several examples of people who are healed, where these two aspects play a role: the aspect of the miracle and the aspect of medicine. (It should not be forgotten that in fact every medical cure is also miracle.) There is a story in the Old Testament about King Hezekiah, who was on his death bed and prayed to be cured. The prophet Isaiah was sent to him and announced that he would live another fifteen years. This was the miracle. Then Isaiah placed a poultice of figs on the King Hezekiah's boil and he was cured. This is the medical aspect (2 Kings 20).

In the New Testament there is a story about a man who was born blind. Jesus spat on the ground, mixed up some dust and saliva, spread this on the man's eyes and then commanded him to wash in the water of Siloam.

The healing of a person who was born blind is a miracle and yet Jesus performed several acts which can also be explained medically. Again there are those two aspects (John 9).

In my view this shows that every medical treatment must be blessed because every true cure comes from heaven. I am not concerned here with the large number of pseudo-cures discovered in our century. We have quickly become adept at suppressing symptoms, so that as soon as one disease has gone, another appears.

2. The reflection in the window pane in the above story is very significant.

It is said that the Devil does not have a reflection. When you stand in front of a mirror and see the Devil standing next to you, you are actually only seeing yourself.

In this case the opposite happened: the woman was standing by a window and saw, not herself, but two angels. Were these her own angels becoming visible for a moment, on her left and right side?

Angels and demons are opposites. We should remember that the Devil is not God's opposite player, for this would give him an all powerful role. He plays opposite the Archangel Michael. The Lord Himself does not have an opposite player.

It is striking to see how varied encounters with angels can be. On the one hand, there are many similarities, but on the other, every experience has something special which is lacking in the first experience. You can learn something new from every story. The following example of a cure is similar to the last one because it also contains these two aspects, but in other respects it is quite different.

35 In 1946 a German woman had a baby boy. At that time conditions in Germany were deplorable. There was widespread hunger, despair, chaos, housing shortages and poverty; it certainly was not an ideal time for having a baby. The woman developed serious mastitis – a very painful condition. Usually the inflammation can be kept under control but in her case abscesses developed and she was ill and feverish for months, so she was not able to look after her baby herself. Psychologically she was also very down during this period.

When it became clear that she was not getting better, her courage did not fail but – in her own words – she "started to praise the Lord and ask Him for help".

One night when the pain and the fever were really bad and she could not sleep a wink she suddenly saw a number of angels standing in front of her bed no more than three metres away, in the morning light. The middle one was wearing a beautiful golden shawl. His garment seemed to be made of a clear shining gold and was so bright that she had to cover her eyes.

She felt totally overwhelmed by this experience, but also comforted. Immediately after this a friend sent her a "Heilpraktikerin". This friend belonged to the same church as she did and had been very sympathetic while she was ill. The naturopath gave her some homoeopathic sulphur (sulphur D6) to take every hour. After eight days all the complaints had disappeared and she was at last able to look after her baby herself.

At first glance there is no connection between the angel with the golden shawl and the remedy which the therapist gave her, but the woman herself did see a connection in this. It was as though the angel had blessed the medicine which she was given shortly afterwards. There is an idea that patients are sent to you from heaven. If they are not cured, they were sent to the wrong place. As you will see, in this case the miracle preceded the medical treatment. I am tremendously pleased that in this heaven chose to bless a homeopathic remedy for the following reason:

There is a new sort of 'monkey roll' story in the Netherlands, though it is not as harmless as that about the angel on the motorway. I would prefer to call it a 'snake roll' story. This story says that homeopathy is forbidden for Christians because this branch of medicine does not come from God but from Satan.

In the past many Christians preferred homeopathic remedies, but now they are exhorted not to turn to this "occult" medicine and to return to the good old-fashioned orthodox practices with safe God fearing remedies such as tranquillizers, birth control pills, sleeping pills and other panacea.

I hope that the above will help doubters to come back to their senses and restore their faith in homeopathy.

Do angels always appear wearing their traditional white clothes with or without sashes and wings? Or – if they don't – do they appear in the form of people dressed in modern clothes, as we saw in a number of stories, so that we can only wonder in retrospect whether they were angels?

Are these the two ways in which they appear to us or is there another possibility?

I have already said that I presume that the appearance is related to the person who has the experience. For example, I could imagine that an angel appearing to a Chinese person might have slanting eyes while an angel appearing to a person from Zambia would be black. To illustrate the great variation which may be expected in the appearance of angels I will give an example here of yet another possibility.

36 This event took place in 1978 and concerns a woman who was suffering from serious depression. She was married and had children. The youngest was eight years old. She was in a state of utter despair and her thoughts were confused.

As is usual in cases of serious depression she had dreadful problems sleeping, which she tried to resolve with pills. Her condition had lasted for eight years and there was no sign of any improvement. The sleeping pills were having less and less effect.

One night when everybody was asleep and she was lying awake all alone, she was in a crisis. She came to the conclusion that it was pointless to live any longer and – in her own words – she wanted to ask God to give Him her life back. She thought that she had not achieved anything in her life. I should add that this is also typical of depression and is usually without foundation.

She had sought professional help but this had been unsuccessful because she could not establish any contact with the people providing assistance. In the loneliness of the night she thought it would be best for her husband if he were liberated from her and she imagined that her older children were old enough to manage. She was only concerned about her youngest child.

Almost rationally she prepared her death. Her confusion was replaced by a deadly logic. Suddenly, there was a "presence" just above her, to the left. It looked like a dark circle which started talking to her without words and she talked back without words. It was the most intense contact she had ever had in her life. The conversation was about comfort, security, and expressing her terrible despair. The contact was full of promise.

After this encounter it was as though she was tucked up

in bed, and she slept wonderfully and deeply for the rest of the night.

The next day she decided that she would never take her own life.

This was certainly an encounter with heaven. Was it an angel? or was it the Lord of Creation Himself?

Again it is striking that the main healing factor was not the conversation itself but the direct contact which was established.

She wrote that this help gave her the great faith that we are not alone in life but that we are cared for with great love and attention.

The butterfly had crawled out of the cocoon. This did not mean that all her problems were solved, but in the following years she had found a support which would never fail her again.

It is curious that immediately after her inner recovery, her husband became seriously stressed and it took him more than two years to recover. Was it the case that for all the years while his wife was ill he had had to cope with dreadful things, and now he was finished, or was there something else the matter? I do not know whether this is the case but I would like to suggest another possibility.

I have often seen a case of a disease being transferred from one member of a family to another. In the case of the woman described above it is possible that she had borne an unresolved problem of her husband's for many years, perhaps entirely unconsciously. Sometimes people consciously take on the problems or suffering of others but that is extremely rare.

Thus it could be that when this woman finally managed to shake off her depression with the help of heaven, the depression settled where it had originally come from, on her husband.

Women are more inclined to take on things from their husbands than vice versa, but this can also happen. There is a true story about a man who was afflicted with serious sciatica. Neither the family doctor nor the specialist could find the cause. Then friends told him that he should go to a manual therapist.

He went and his wife accompanied him. However, the manual therapist could not find anything wrong and the wife asked him what he was doing exactly.

The man showed her her back and explained that sometimes a vertebra could be out of place causing sciatica.
Suddenly he stopped and said: "There is nothing wrong
with your husband's back, but did you know that there is
something wrong with yours? Could I put it right
because it will certainly trouble you?"
The woman said that she had fallen down the stairs six
months before and wondered whether that could have
been the cause, though she did not have any pain.
The manual therapist thought that this was quite possible
for it often happened after a fall. Then he manipulated
the woman's spine and just as the vertebra which was out
of place clicked into place, her husband shouted out with
pain and was instantly cured of his sciatica.
Husbands and wives are often a closer unit than they
realise and the expression in Genesis that they are "one
flesh" is often literally true. In the example of the woman
with the circle we saw that this time there was no contact
between a person and a "ceremonial" angel but between
a person and an inhabitant of heaven who manifested
himself as a mathematical figure, a circle. In her condition
this was probably best because sometimes patients suffering from depression are so withered psychologically that
they are reduced to a dot. The circle is exactly the symbol
that can help such a person to expand and rediscover the
fullness of life.

ANGELS AND DEATH

The last thing to happen at home is death.
Thus we can certainly expect to see angels on the threshold to the next world.
Here is a story which may not be a real story about angels
but is nevertheless about such a threshold experience, a
"hole in the net", through which exchanges take place.

37 Some people have such an unequal amount of suffering to deal with that you occasionally have the
feeling that suffering is unfairly divided. The woman in
this story grew up with a mother who never loved her.
The reason was simple: she should have been a boy.
A child who grows up without love has enough sadness
and security to last a lifetime. As though this were not

enough she was also struck by a serious infection, and ended up in a wheelchair.

By this time she was already married but her marriage was also very painful. Her mother fell in love with her husband, which obviously led to enormous tension and finally her husband left her because he could not cope with her handicap.

At last her mother was dying. She sat by her death-bed holding her hand.

Even at the last I think she still cherished that one great illusion, that her mother would tell her, even if it were just once: "My child, I love you".

The woman did actually open her eyes just before she died, looked at her daughter with intense hatred and uttered just two words as she breathed her last breath, and then she said: "You wretch!"

This was just a small part of the woman's heavy lot. I will spare you the rest.

The reason that I included this story in the book is this. The mother died in 1957 and about 20 years later she suddenly appeared to her daughter in a vision. She asked her for forgiveness and said: "Was it so terrible what I did to you? If you forgive me, never say that it wasn't so bad, because it is very difficult to ask for forgiveness, even from yourself".

The woman then did the right thing. She said: "It's terrible what you did, but I forgive you. How else could I ever ask for forgiveness myself?"

C.S. Lewis wrote a penetrating analysis of the sentence in Our Lord's Prayer: "Forgive us our trespasses as we forgive them that trespass against us."

In the first place he emphasizes the fact that forgiveness is conditional for it depends on the way in which we forgive others. However, he then asks what forgiveness is. He answers this question by saying that forgiveness is forgiving those things that are inexcusable.

The striking thing is that this woman's mother was clearly afraid that her daughter would try to make excuses for her behaviour. It is as though she clearly realized that she could not be redeemed, unless it was clearly stated that there was no excuse for her behaviour. Only then could she be truly delivered and be free.

It was clever of her daughter to understand this intuitively. She did not try to make excuses for her mother's behaviour but adopted the only correct position – in the light of eternity – viz., that her behaviour had been abominable but she wished to forgive her mother nevertheless. This gives this story its ring of truth. It is not something which took place only in the daughter's soul. There were two people, one who is still alive and one who is no longer here, opposite each other. They made contact through the holes in the net and resolved some unfinished business. Both emerged from this better and purified.

The Bible warns seriously against making contact with the dead through a medium. Mosaic law is very clear about this and when Saul tried to break this law and sought contact with the medium of Endor, this cost him his life (1 Samuel 28).

However, the spontaneous occurrence of contact with someone who has died is not forbidden anywhere. In this context the incident involving Moses and Elijah during the Transfiguration on the Mount springs to mind (Matthew 17). It should be realized that there is a clear boundary between calling up the dead, which is forbidden, and a spontaneous meeting with the dead, and this is quite understandable.

A spontaneous meeting with a person who has died – like mercy from heaven – is sanctioned, but the decision to discover a secret before the time is right, is condemned. Isn't this often the case in our daily life?

We are constantly concerned with these situations, especially during our festivals. We like surprises, for example, preparing a festive meal or what is in presents at St. Nicholas or Christmas. What could that big parcel be?

Why do we do this? It is because that we know that the discovery of a secret at the right moment gives the greatest possible joy? We should allow God to keep back things which He wishes to show us as a surprise in His own good time. This always concerns a metamorphosis of our soul, not a sort of celestial welfare state. If this were the case we would become so blasé that we would die of boredom. We will look at a few stories in which angels did appear at a death bed.

38 There was a woman lying in a small room in a hospital.

She was 72 years old and two of her children, a brother and sister, were sitting by her bed because she was dying. The son was reading quietly, and the daughter was looking at her mother in the way that people commonly look at their loved ones who will soon be gone. The patient was lying absolutely still, her eyes shut.

Suddenly her daughter saw an angel floating into the room at some speed. He did not come through a window, nor through the door, but appeared through the wall about three metres up. When he arrived at the bedside of the dying woman, he knelt down by her bed on one knee. She saw her mother opening her eyes, the angel and her mother looked at each other, and the old woman said: 'Yes.' Then the angel disappeared.

His presence was very strong, and gave the woman a safe feeling. She also felt that this was not at all strange, but almost self-evident.

The next day her mother died. This is how a good person dies. It does not always have to be the next of kin who sees these things.

39 In June 1983 a woman was lying in a ward in a hospital in Haarlem. She had to have a gallstone operation, but first a number of examinations had to be carried out. That is why she was allowed to go home for the weekend and she was looking forward to this. On Friday morning, the day she was allowed to leave, she woke up very early. Suddenly she saw a large angel floating diagonally opposite her over the bed of another patient in the ward. She asked the girl lying next to her whether she could see it too, but she could not. The angel continued to float above the bed and when her family came to fetch her at 10 o'clock, she could still see the angel. She very consciously said goodbye to the woman as she was convinced that she would not see her alive again. In fact the woman died on Sunday morning.

This story is another example of angels which are not visible to everyone. Sometimes two or more people see the same thing, but usually one can see an angel while another person who is there as well, does not see it. This clearly shows that such an apparition, though it is

concerned with a dying person, is yet of personal significance to the person who sees it. Anyone who sees an
angel is always intensely involved – this person is actually
intended to have the experience. In matters of heaven
there is no such thing as random perception.

40 The following story came to me second-hand.
A man from Germany wrote to me that he had
lost his father at a very early age. His father and mother
had married in 1909 and his father died in 1914.
When his mother was at his father's death-bed he
breathed his last, a long deep sigh, after which there was
no more breathing.
Exactly at that moment a large angel dressed in white
stood by her husband's bed. His mother was deeply
moved and called out: "What's that?" Then the angel
came away from the floor, floated up and disappeared
through the ceiling.
She believes that he took her husband's soul with him.
She had told her son that she was quite lucid and that she
would take an oath that the story was true. According to
Jewish tradition the Angel Gabriel gives instruction to
souls about to be born about the earth where they will
soon arrive, but he also promises these souls that he will
fetch them at the end of life. Perhaps this is what the
woman saw.

41 Doctors are also aware of the proximity of angels.
In 1987 a German gynaecologist was by her husband's death-bed. He had cancer of the pancreas, and his
suffering had been long and painful. This is a very difficult time both for the immediate family and for the
patient, a period of great trials.
When her husband was sinking further and further away
and she herself was almost exhausted, she suddenly felt
a great warm peaceful hand on her neck radiating
strength. The fingers were surprisingly long. The hand
moved her gently forward and enabled her to support
her husband until he breathed his last.
The last case I will mention reveals an aspect that would
almost be comical if it were not concerned with a dying
man.

42 In 1984 I received a letter from a very sad woman who had not yet come to terms with her husband's death. She thought about it day and night. Her husband had died of lung cancer and with the help of a wise priest he had been able to reconcile himself to his death.

A month before he died the following incident occurred. Two angels came to his bed and said to him: "We have come to fetch you."

Then her husband said: "No, that would not be very convenient at the moment, because we are about to move house."

The angels replied: "Alright then, we will come back for you after the move."

The husband told this story first to the priest and then to his wife. The couple moved into the house and then he died.

Incredible? I don't think so. I think he was a good person who wanted to show his wife that he loved her one last time by moving into the new house with her.

Doing good can save a person from death or, as in this case, delay death a little longer.

This brings us to the end of angels in the home. It shows us that it is not necessary to travel to distant gurus or great masters in order to gain wisdom and insight. The greatest and most wonderful adventures happen in our own bedrooms, kitchens or gardens. If we simply carry on with our lives, we will emerge from our chrysalis at the right time and the butterfly will appear.

If you are one of those people who never sees an angel, do not be sad. It means that there is no need for you to see one. But live your life so that they would be happy to be in your home.

CHAPTER 4

CHILDREN AND ANGELS

We live in an age when Christianity is disappearing on a large scale.

The world has become a hard, businesslike place.

Television drags our children towards adulthood much too quickly.

The mystery which should always be part of childhood is replaced by scientific explanations and technology. And yet you can still see heaven in children's eyes because heaven will not allow itself to be completely repressed. The world may have become largely dechristianized but children have not.

However, they are in danger.

In the days before the disappearance of faith there was still a God in heaven and angels when you went to sleep. Admittedly the world was always full of threats but fortunately there were still miracles then.

However, when man started to believe that the visible world is the only true world, he closed the way to heaven. You cannot do this without punishment. The underworld starts to rumble straightaway, and ancient chained gods throw off their shackles. Jung wrote that under Hitler the German people had fallen into the stranglehold of one of these ancient gods, and thought he could identify Wodan, the ancient god of hunting.

One might also say that the whole of the industrialized

world has fallen into the power of the ancient god of the Underworld, Pluto, the great lord of technology, the power of subterranean fire.

It is striking that fire has played an increasingly important role in the history of mankind since the beginning of this process of dechristianization, which really got underway in the French Revolution. This can be seen from the invention of the internal combustion engine to nuclear explosions.

Man must worship something – this is how he was created – and that is why we now kneel down before the State, science, the welfare state. Alternative saviours appear by the dozen and have presented us with entirely new doctrines of salvation. In some cases these have been political saviours. Their idolatrous nature can be recognized from the fact that they have huge photographs made of themselves, 10 metres high. Just think of Mao, Stalin, Saddam Hussein. Every idol and every pseudo-saviour demands uncompromising devotion. Anyone who does not comply is tortured and killed.

In some cases they were pseudo-religious saviours who incited their followers to commit suicide and become prostitutes. What happens to the soul of a child who grows up in a state where he has learned to worship the 'Great Helmsman'? What do we do ourselves to the souls of our children when we allow them to learn at school that their ancestors were a sort of ape?

We look down with contempt on Ancient people who sacrificed new-born children in a burning idolatrous image while the screams of the child were drowned by the loud banging of drums. We are much too enlightened to worship the Moloch.

But is this really true? Has everyone forgotten the film *The Silent Scream* in which we see how a foetus opens its mouth wide in a silent scream of terror just before being ripped out of the womb by a doctor performing an abortion? Is this not really worshipping Moloch?

How dare we look down on the grisly practices of Ancient people? We are not a jot better ourselves, though we wrap our unwholesome deeds up in sterile operating gowns and scientific sounding words. Why have we become so blasé that we no longer read to our children from the Good Book which has served our culture for twenty centuries? Could all the great minds for whom it was a source of strength, have been so wrong?

Why are children no longer told about David and Goliath, Queen Esther and about the Good Shepherd before they go to sleep and why do they watch Ninja Turtles on t.v. instead?

Their immortal souls are fed with illusions and must be hungry. Their souls are like their physical bodies which have become rotten with all the synthetic foods produced in factories.

What atheist communism failed to do, we have succeeded in achieving in our welfare state: we have finally managed to turn our children into heathens.

Desiderius Erasmus (1469 – 1536) once said: "Man is not born as man, he is made into man".

We have succeeded in removing the element of 'making man' from our pattern of childrearing. In the twentieth century we make things instead of souls. We produce a tremendous amount of material without any substance.

Heathenism finally seemed to have won for good when suddenly, at the end of the twentieth century, the dividing wall between this world and the other world seemed to crack. Not only was the Berlin Wall torn down, but the apparently indestructible dividing wall erected by nineteenth century materialism, also started to crumble. What is happening, and why?

Before starting with children I would like to make an apology.

First of all, this question: "Has Jesus Christ really been abolished?" I spoke to an Anglican vicar who said to me quite seriously that in the past, Jesus Christ was the great leader, but that he had continued to evolve in the fields of heaven, and that there were other spirits to help us now.

I have rarely been so shocked.

Here, I would like to state quite clearly that I believe what the Bible says. Not because the Bible is aesthetically pleasing or because it is philosophically interesting or because it teaches great moral lessons. You can learn all these things from the many other holy books written by the many different people of the world. The reason that I believe what the Bible says, is that I am convinced it is true. I entirely agree with Lewis when he says – I am not quoting him literally – that there are two possibilities: either what Jesus says about Himself is true in which case it is best to take it into account, or what He says is so absurd that we do not need to take it into account.

After a lengthy study and comparisons with other religious systems as well as a great deal of self study, I have come to the conclusion that the Bible is true and that when I do not understand it, that is my fault. Therefore, when the Bible says that there is one mediator between God and men, the man Christ Jesus (1 Tim. 2:5), I believe that is true. For me this also means that this mediator has not departed with the process of dechristianization. Rather, it has been sent out of the door and that is why there is a very strange prophecy in The Revelation of St John. At the beginning of the book we find the seven epistles to the seven communities in Asia. These seven communities are a prophecy of the church history of Europe. We are living now in the era of the church of Laodicea, the church which has become luke-warm and to this community Jesus said: "See, I am knocking at the door."

It couldn't be clearer. In our time, He is outside the door. But if there is one loud and clear message in the New Testament it is that He will come back.

I believe that the cracks which are appearing so clearly in the wall we erected so diligently together, indicate that the King of angels is getting ready for His return. His servants have already been sighted here and there. They are the precursors of the royal procession. Who could identify these preparations better than the little children who have left heaven so recently that they still have a special bond with the angels. Below, I will give an anthology from the many letters I have received about children and angels. As far as possible I have tried to include all the stories about children in this chapter. I have not managed to do so altogether simply because children have a tendency to ignore boundaries and wander everywhere. This is why children were mentioned in the very first chapters and it would not surprise me at all if one or two escaped into the last chapters, but most of them can be found here. I will start with the following reflections. Most of the experiences of angels involving children were written to me when the children concerned had grown up. The experience was usually related with the introductory words: "When I was a child something very extraordinary happened to me".

The question arises whether such memories are reliable. In my experience many things from the past become rather vague: even the clearest dreams, even the finest memories lose their clarity in time. Admittedly some people have a better memory than others and one person may be better at capturing an image than another, but eventually time leaves its mark on all of us. When we look at the photographs of our children as babies or toddlers it is sometimes difficult to work out which child it is. Sometimes you don't know whether you remember something from your own youth because it is recorded in a photograph or in a diary, or because it is really a childhood memory.

Only those events which are intensely and consciously experienced, and which were accompanied by strong emotions remain etched on our memories. No matter how old we become they remain clear and fresh. Everyone has memories like these and the strange thing is that the events concerned are by no means those we considered to be 'important' ourselves. For example, I hardly remember the 'important' moment when I was granted a doctorate and had to take the oath but I remember as though it were only yesterday that I was sitting on a bright green sward of grass by a flowing stream in the south of England with rhododendrons flowering profusely all around me. I can still hear the water babbling and see the purple abundance of the tall rhododendron bushes.

The more conscious you are at the time of an experience, the stronger the memory of that experience will be. Really good memories arise from times of heightened consciousness. This reveals that on the whole our consciousness is rather mediocre. Most of our experiences take place while we are not fully awake and they soon assume a dreamlike character in our memory. This can be so extreme that we may say of a memory: did that really happen or was it a dream? Childhood experiences of angels have the clarity of peak experiences and therefore indicate that the events really took place.

We would do well to believe what we are told about

these experiences. I recall one particularly sad case.

Freud fairly often treated young women who described incestuous situations to him. He described these terrible recollections engraved on their memory as the 'secret desire' of the little girls to have intercourse with their father, and not as a real and terrible experience. Some people have accused Freud of treating them in this way because the fathers concerned had to pay the bill. In any case, the result was that Freud's followers faithfully continued to interpret every incestuous experience of their patients as shameless desires from childhood. In this way they were responsible for an unimaginable amount of damage and suffering. Not only had the patient been abused as a child, and was therefore full of feelings of guilt and insecurity, but in addition, the patient was told that these things had merely been fantasies. What had actually amounted to the rape of a small child was described in therapy as a sort of perversion of that child. The patient was condemned to even greater loneliness.

It was not until the 1980s, i.e., eighty or ninety years after Freud had repressed his findings on incest so insistently, that it was found that the patients had actually been telling the truth all the time, and that incest occurred on an almost unbelievable scale. I can imagine there are people who would, for personal (psychological) reasons, like to relegate the stories of children's personal experiences with angels to the realms of the imagination and wish fulfilment. The existence of angels is rather difficult to swallow for people who have grown up in the materialist world.

However, the clarity, penetration and lasting quality of the memories about angels are a testimony to their authenticity, even if they occurred very early in life.

Before I start, I would like to state one other thing:

the word 'angel' means 'messenger', but you will have noticed that up to now the angels have given few messages, or will they do so in the following stories? I have gradually come to realize that an angel does not usually *bring* a message in the sense of a particular announcement. This does happen from time to time, but only in a minority of cases. The angel is actually the message himself. His appearance is the message that heaven is intensely concerned with us, and that God cares for us like a father for his children.

ANGELS APPEAR TO CHILDREN

43 Some children do not seem to belong entirely to this world. They have dreamy eyes and seem to be sensitive to things which other children do not understand. Catharine was such a girl. She was a sweet child, but very lonely. She had strong intuitive powers which enabled her to understand animals and people in a way you don't usually find in seven or eight-year-old children. Fortunately, there were two people in her life whom she loved very much: her favorite aunt, her father's sister, and her maternal grandfather. These people gave her warmth and understanding. Then disaster struck in her young life when her aunt and grandfather died within a short space of time. The child was desperate and lonelier than ever.

One day she was visiting her grandmother, and suddenly she had the feeling that there was someone in the next room. She was alone, and she knew that the other room must be empty. At first she was very wary, and did not dare enter. But she soon had a clear feeling that whatever, or whoever was there meant her well. Therefore she went into the other room and stood stock still.

Just in front of her, about one metre above the ground, there were two floating figures who looked like people. They radiated great love. She hardly dared to look at them, but then she heard these beings speaking within herself. They told her that they understood how difficult things were for her, and then they gave her a short summary of the life ahead. They showed her the way she should follow.

After this 'conversation' she was tremendously relieved. Her fears fell away and she was able to continue her life full of courage. She kept this event deep in her heart, and it was only when she was an adult married woman that she first spoke to anyone about it.

As is the case with most sensitive children, she had a great deal more illness and insecurity to contend with in her youth, but the two angels had told her that her new

life would take a turn for the better when she was twenty-
three, and that is what happened.

Thus these angels did have a message to give but their
appearance was at least as important as the message itself.
This lonely child, who had just lost two key figures in
her life suddenly knew that she was looked after and that
she did not have to go on on her own. She had lost two
loved ones and two angels were ready for her – that was
the true message behind the words.

In her letter the woman once again emphasized that all
this happened while she was fully conscious.

You could argue that there was an obvious reason for the
appearance of these angels. The following story,
described by a woman of forty, is rather different.

44 Just imagine an ordinary Dutch living room.
There is a little girl of seven looking at a book
with pictures of rabbits, her elbows leaning on the table.
Her little brother is playing on the floor. There is no one
else in the room. Suddenly she turns round and sees an
angel standing only one metre away, next to the heater.
He is dressed in a light blue garment and has a beautiful
face and she realizes straight away that he is not made
of flesh and blood. The angel and the child look at one
another, they both smile and the little girl's eyes fill
with tears of emotion. Then the angel nods a few times
and suddenly turns into a thick mist which dissolves
right in front of her eyes, until there is nothing left to
see. Her little brother did not see anything and is still
playing. I wrote back to this woman and asked her
why an angel had appeared to her and she told me a
strange story.

Unlike most people who have an experience of angels,
she had told her mother what had happened straightaway
and she related the experience to the following event.

The mother had grown up in a different country where
she had been friendly with the boy next door. They had
the same interests and hobbies. When he was twenty-
three, the boy contracted tuberculosis and at that time
most people still died from this disease. While he was ill
they talked a great deal about the problems of life and
death and about the question of whether there was life
after this life. One day the boy said: "I promise you that

after my death I will let you know whether there is a hereafter."

However, she did not agree to this. She thought this confirmation was unnecessary and advised him against it. Meanwhile she married and became pregnant with the child who saw the angel. The boy next door died after a time and two days later she gave birth to her daughter.

When she had told this story to her child, she said: "I think that he sent the confirmation of life after death to you, because I didn't want it. I believe that when the angel nodded, he meant: "Yes! There is life after death!" I am glad that I asked for this explanation for otherwise this surprising solution would not have come to light. The mother and daughter were touched by heaven at the same time.

Again the angel here was a messenger. Sometimes experiences with angels can also be stimulated by events in the outside world.

45 A girl of nine had a teacher at school who told her one day that you can often see angels and that you can even see Jesus. Suddenly she saw a great, shining light that completely blinded her. The child herself started to shine as well and her astonished teacher asked her what was the matter but she did not dare to say.

This was an extremely important moment in her life which was a great comfort to her, particularly during the time she spent in a Japanese camp during the war.

This is another striking example of a really important moment in someone's life taking place in secret.

46 A five-year-old girl always felt that when her mother sang a particular song, it was a very special moment. Usually her mother would sing when she was working in the kitchen. The refrain went: There are angels all around us, there are angels all around us!

As soon as her mother started singing this song the girl would take her own little chair and go and sit outside. Then she would see angels floating towards her in long white garments. She shut her eyes quickly, folded her hands and felt their soft garments stroking her forehead and her left cheek. When her mother stopped singing, the angels were gone.

As the rest of the letter which she wrote to me when she had grown up shows, she had always thought in images as a child. Some people think in words, others in images. People who think in images can hardly imagine that someone who thinks in words does not see anything when he is thinking.

Did the child see angels or did she have 'images' of angels or does the distinction between these even exist in a five-year-old? In that case are the images true in many cases? It just depends on which way you look at it.

HEALING

This follows on from earlier stories, for we came across the miraculous cure of a child in the Christmas story.

47 First, here is a very short story. A woman remembers being very ill once when she was a child. She had a very high temperature for a long time. Then two hands appeared at the foot of her bed and immediately she said: "Tomorrow I will be better." This is what happened. This story is particularly important because there is a Jewish tradition which says that you should never stand at the foot of a sick person's bed because that place is reserved for the guardian angel.

Although most people whose experiences are included in this book, told or wrote to me about their experiences personally, I have occasionally made an exception to illustrate particular points more clearly.

Someone from Germany sent me an article written by a masseur. One day, when this man was massaging a woman, she told him the following story. (Massage is well known for loosening the tongue as well as relaxing the muscles.)

As a child she had always loved flowering heather. In fact she always retained her love for the erica plant.

When she was seven she contracted a serious case of pneumonia. She was in a critical condition, because this took place in a time before antibiotics. Her mother was desperately worried and slept on a camp-bed next to her. In the middle of the night the mother suddenly awoke because the child was loudly calling for her. She sat bolt upright and saw a shining figure standing at the foot of the girl's bed, wearing a long white garment and carrying a large bush of flowering heather in his hand. The figure looked quietly at her sleeping daughter. The angel and the child's bed were surrounded by a glow of light. After about ten seconds the apparition dissolved and the room was in darkness again.

The next morning the family doctor was amazed to find that the child was cured. He listened to the mother's story but did not really believe it. The child herself, now the woman who told the masseur the story, did not remember any of this.

Therefore, the angel also stood in his right place at the foot of the bed in this story.

It is interesting to note that in the Scottish highlands a very potent cough medicine is made from flowering heather and honey (Melly Uyldert).

The child got better and the heather was involved in this but I don't know how the angel cured her with the heather.

However, we have already seen that heaven has a predilection for simple, good remedies.

It is striking that most of these stories about childhood experiences with angels were told to me by women. I am convinced that there are just as many boys who have had such experiences, but men are much more afraid of losing face and therefore tend to talk about them less. The next story was also told to me by a woman. When she wrote to me she was 75 years old.

The First World War broke out in 1914 and all the children in The Hague were vaccinated against smallpox.

This woman was four years old at the time. Unfortunately, she was one of the children who contracted encephalitis from the vaccination and she soon fell into a coma. After four days the family doctor told her mother: "She will be in crisis tonight and then she will not last long."

Her mother was sitting by her bed that night when the little girl suddenly stretched out. Her mother and father quickly went to her side because they thought the end had come.

What was actually happening to the child? She remembers that she was on her way somewhere when suddenly there was an angel before her. He was in the form of a twelve-year-old, completely dressed in white and very beautiful. He was standing under a magnificent bright blue sky.

The girl immediately regained consciousness and called out: "Oh, Mummy, I was almost an angel!" She had a crystal clear memory of this experience. She also notes that she had never been to a Sunday school or to church, so that her soul was not prepared for such an experience.

Once again we find that, very curiously, the angel did not do anything. He was just there. The healing was the result of the encounter. The woman then survived this disease, which is usually fatal, without any after-effects. Angels are the hands and feet of God. His close proximity drives out any sickness. The woman in the New Testament who had been bleeding for twelve years, also knew this. She secretly but very quickly touched His robe and was cured (Matthew 9:21).

The last case of the girl's encounter with an angel obviously was not an example of an experience which took place while she was fully conscious. Some people might say that she had encephalitis, an inflammation of the brain, so hallucinations were to be expected.

However, we should not forget that the child was cured at the very last moment!

It is important to guard against belonging to the group of people who mocked the Apostles when they were filled with the Holy Ghost and spoke in many tongues on Whit Sunday in Jerusalem, saying: "They have drunk too much sweet wine!"

In order to avoid a dry recounting of facts I will include a second Christmas story here.

The south west of Florida is not only an area where alligators swim in marshes – there is also more open countryside with brushwood, palm trees and shallow ditches.

It had been a hot damp December and was almost Christmas. It had rained in the night and a gentle breeze was blowing from the south east, bringing humid air from the ocean, but it was dry and the sun was shining.

A boy and a dog were walking through the quiet, isolated landscape. The boy's name was Mark Durrance. He was 12 years old and he was wearing jeans, a T-shirt and strong leather boots. He had fair hair and bright blue eyes. An air-gun was slung over his shoulder.

His dog Bobo was between a poodle and an alsatian in size. Mark liked walking with Bobo. With his air-gun over his shoulders and his dog by his side he felt like a lone woodsman, part of the tradition of the land.

When Mark and Bobo were returning home he suddenly saw a beautifully coloured bird in a fan palm. The tree was on the other side of a ditch and as he wanted to know what sort of bird it was, he took a run up and jumped over the ditch, his eyes still on the bird.

He landed on something which seemed to roll over under his right foot and immediately felt such an explosion of pain that it was as though someone was hacking his foot with an axe. At first he seemed to be slightly anaesthetized, and then the pain was overpowering and seemed to shoot up his lower leg like a scorching fire. He looked down and to his horror saw the enormous head of a rattlesnake wrapped round his right foot.

Rattlesnakes can be more than two and a half metres long and this was a gigantic specimen. The razor-sharp venomous teeth had bored straight through the leather boot and had unfortunately pierced the big vein which runs along the top of the foot. The snake did not let go – it was probably stuck in the leather and it injected all its venom straight into Mark's foot.

There are many different sorts of poisonous snakes. For example, the venom of the cobra is a so-called neuro-toxin, a poison which paralyses the victim. In contrast, the rattlesnake has a venom which makes the blood clot and destroys the capillary veins, a so-called haemotoxin. The victim is often able to walk a few yards but then falls down. To get its prey, the snake then locates the place where its victim has fallen with a separate olfactory organ, the 'organ of Jacobson'. Unlike the copperhead, which is also found in that area, the rattlesnake does not usually attack human beings. When it is irritated it usually lifts the tip of its tail and makes a rattling sound as a warning. However, this snake had not had time to do so, because Mark had unexpectedly jumped on it.

When Bobo saw his master's danger he attacked the snake
furiously but it was only when he shook the reptile's head
between his teeth, that the monster let go and slithered
into the bushes.

Mark was 140 meters from home and he knew no one
would be able to hear him. He would have to try and
get home very carefully. He must not move too quickly
because the faster you walk the faster the poison moves
to the heart. But when he had taken a few steps he realized
that he could not go on. The pain was overwhelming.
All his strength ebbed away and everything around him
started to blur. The destruction of his body had already
started. The red blood cells were coagulating, the capillary veins were bursting, his heartbeat became irregular,
his respiration speeded up and was superficial. It looked
as though Mark's hour had come.

The Durrance house was situated in an isolated spot on
the side of low hills. Bobby Durrance, Mark's father,
was pruning the bushes in the front garden when Buddy,
the oldest son, came running up screaming: "Dad,
Mark's been bitten by a snake!".

Bobby, a strong, athletic man who had worked as
an oilrigger for years, ran into the house and found
Mark lying on the floor unconscious. Debby, Mark's
mother, was standing next to him, wringing her
hands.

"What happened?" asked Bobby.

"Mark just appeared at the door and said, very quietly,
that he had been bitten by a snake. Then he fell to the
floor unconscious and had terrible convulsions" sobbed
Debby. Then they noticed that the room was filled with
a penetrating musky smell which they had also noticed
when a pet had been bitten by a rattlesnake.

As quickly as they could they took off Mark's boots and
found a nasty, purplish red swelling on his right foot.
The swelling was the size of a grapefruit and they realized
that Mark only had a chance if they took him to hospital
as quickly as possible. The house did not have a tele-
phone. They quickly put a tourniquet around the right
leg, not realizing that the poison which had got into the
vein had already spread a long way, and ran to their open
van with Mark in their arms.

While Mark's breathing grew weaker they put their foot

down and drove to the clinic which was 27 km away. Debby pressed her face against her son's and felt his breathing getting weaker and weaker. She could only pray the following prayers. "Though I walk through the valley of the shadow of death, I will fear no evil for thou art with me." (Psalm 23:4). The former Dutch Queen Wilhelmina commented on this verse in her beautiful little book: *De Heer is mijn herder* (The Lord is my Shepherd).

She explains that this verse from David's psalm refers to the deep, dark chasm in the mountains between Jerusalem and Jericho. This area was particularly dangerous at night. Nowadays there is a metalled road which goes down to the Dead Sea, but in David's day it was a road full of deep crevasses and abysses and it was notorious among the shepherds.

Debby repeated this verse to herself again and again as they sped along with the dying child.

A mile and a half from the clinic the engine overheated, began to boil and the van stopped. Bobby jumped out, desperately waving his arms but everyone drove past him. Then he took Mark from Debby's arms, carried him to the middle of the road and held the limp child, almost dead, like a flag.

It was a Haitian farm labourer, who did not pass him by, but braked and stopped. He did not speak any English but saw at a glance what was the matter, took the family in his car and raced to the clinic as they showed him the way.

When they arrived Mark's condition was so serious that there was little the doctors could do. He was almost dead and no longer breathing. He was immediately placed on a respirator, put on a drip, and was then taken by ambulance to the big hospital ten miles away where more could be done for him.

The surgeon, Michael Nycan, was just washing his boat when his bleeper gave the alarm. Mark was injected with large amounts of antidote but they did not take effect. His kidneys had almost stopped functioning and his breathing could only be kept going artificially. He was in a deep coma and blood was constantly seeping from his ears, mouth and eyes for this strange poison, on the one hand, causes clotting, but on the other, also thins the blood. He looked terrible, his eyelids were swollen and deformed and blood seeped constantly through the cracks that remained. In the course of twenty-four hours he was given eighteen blood transfusions.

The whole of the next day he spent hovering between life and death. His right leg was in danger of becoming gangrenous with the swelling and deep incisions had to be made to make circulation possible.

All night Debby prayed out loud by the side of her comatose son for though he was in a coma she thought it might get through to him anyway.

This was not such a bad thought for we now know that patients in a coma and sometimes even patients undergoing an operation, can hear conversations around them.

To everyone's surprise Mark started to regain consciousness on the third day. When he was completely conscious, he related with remarkable clarity how he had jumped on the rattlesnake. The doctors and nurses who came to listen burst out laughing when he begged his father's pardon for being so careless. Everyone was relieved that he had not suffered any brain damage. Later, when all the hospital staff had left his room only his parents remained by his bedside. Debby wiped his swollen forehead and held his swollen hand in hers.

"There is one thing I don't understand," said Bob. "How in heaven's name did you get home?"

The question seemed to hang in the air between them for a moment as they sat together in silence and the sun shone into the sickroom. Then Mark began his story: "I seemed to be nailed to the ground and really couldn't move another step, and then a man dressed in white suddenly appeared before me. He lifted me up and carried me home across the field. He had a low, friendly voice and as he walked he told me I would be sick but that I needn't be afraid because I would live.

"Then we were home. He walked the thirteen steps to the front door with me and put me down and then he rose up to heaven before my eyes. I knew that it was God. I just managed to take one step inside and say that I had been bitten by a snake and after that I don't remember anything until I woke up today."

Mark told this story in a very quiet and restrained way.

There is no natural explanation for how he managed to cover the 140 metres across country.

He had several skin-grafts on his foot where he had lost a lot of tissue, but he was eventually completely healed.

Sometimes we speak metaphorically of someone in difficulty being carried by God, but Mark will go through life with the knowledge that this happened to him in a literal sense.

The reader might like to know which parts of this story are true.

In fact, the *whole* story is true. Some of you may have read about this incident already in *The Best of Readers Digest*, published in October 1988. It was written by Henry Hurt.

The only thing I made up is that it took place in December because I happened to tell this story on Christmas Eve. I also made up details about the weather as I don't know whether rattlesnakes live outside in the middle of winter, so the weather had to be good.

The remarkable thing about this story apart from the incredible miracle – is that the boy was saved by being carried home. After this a great deal was left up to the parents, a Haitian farm worker, and the whole medical staff. There is a perfect balance. When these people had to resolve problems themselves, Our Lord left it to them. When they were unable to, He intervened himself.

Again there was the remarkable combination of a miracle and human action – a combination which often occurs. There is the example of the toddler who ran onto the motorway. The angel child held the little girl until the parents reached her.

This is also a strong argument against the Sunday school teacher who taught children that there was no need for them to watch out when they crossed the road because the angels would take care of them. (This really happened.) In our lives we are all required to make the best possible effort and anything beyond that may be granted by heaven.

Therefore, one of the great enigmas of life is why heaven does not do this very often.

One more thing about Mark. Ancient tales from the East often tell of someone who has a narrow escape from death. A stone just misses someone's head or a snake just fails to bite someone. This happens because the person who escapes did an unexpected good deed and thereby fell behind on his personal schedule. Then he just missed the stone or the snake.

Yet the moral of the story is that the snake (or stone) had been waiting for him/her ever since the beginning of creation, and a good deed saved the person's life.

In the East there is a strong conviction that we are not simply created but that circumstances are created with us. In this sense it could be said that the rattlesnake had been lying in wait to bite Mark from the beginning of creation. It seemed as though he landed on it accidentally but that was not the case. In actual fact it was that snake which introduced him to Our Lord.

This means that the story has an extra special meaning. There was a snake at the beginning of our history.

If only Eve had not listened to it!

Yet the Jewish doctrine teaches that the Bible does not describe how things should have been, but how they are. Eve had to listen, or the story could not have proceeded. Again I would like to emphasize in this book that the important thing in this world is for our immortal soul to awaken. It is this soul which is meant for resurrection. Just note the wonderful structure of this story.

First there is a hunter with his dog. The dog is a creature which takes us out into nature. There is the excitement of the hunt. This is how our life starts. We forget that we are here to do something other than hunt.

Then a strange bird attracts our attention. This is reminiscent of the story about the bird which you chase all your life only to find it on your own roof in the end. This symbolic tale indicates that man must remain restless until he has discovered the true meaning of life.

Then there is a great crisis. In real life this often takes place around the age of 40. Depression, ill health, an accident. You discover that you are not who you thought you were.

This is the stage which was expressed with incomparable beauty in the book of Jonah, when he prayed to God inside the huge fish: "The waters compassed me about, even to the soul: the depth closed me round about, the weeds were wrapped about my head. I went down to the

bottom of the mountains; the earth with her bars was
about me for ever." (Jonah 2:5, 6).

Then we discover to our great surprise that we do not
belong to ourselves. That we do not have to be so
ambitious arranging everything, but that it is God who
carries us and loves us and leads us.

This is how Mark was carried home. Jonah said: "Yet
hast though brought up my life from corruption, O Lord
my God." (Jonah 2:6).

This is not the end of the story. On the contrary, it is
really the beginning. Mark experiences the pain, the illness, the operations and has a whole life before him, but
as a new person, and this is what it all started with. In
this way his story is more than just another story about
angels. It has become the archetype of the pattern of life
as it should be. Stories about angels and stories about
heaven are never sensational stories.

Through the astonishing appearance of this sort of
experience, it is possible to distinguish an ever more
profound significance which gives it an entirely new
aspect.

An experience of heaven is at the same time real and
symbolic. There are more and more meanings to be discovered. It is sometimes said that if you explain certain
Biblical events symbolically, this raises the question
whether they really happened. For example, if the journey of Israel through the desert is explained as the journey
of mankind from material reality to the realms of heaven,
did this exodus really happen? Or if the healing in the
New Testament of a man who was born blind symbolizes
the fact that we are all born blind and that the eyes of our
spirituality must be opened during our lifetime, did Jesus
really heal a man who was born blind?

Obviously there was a real exodus and obviously a man
who was born blind was healed. But at the same time
these events also mean something to each of us or they
would just be wonderful stories about distant places and
ancient times. It is precisely from the stories about angels
which take place in our midst *in the present* that we can
learn how real events and symbols coincide.

As I have once again broken my intention of telling
stories first hand as far as possible, I will continue in this
forbidden vein and relate the following story from *The*

News, Maple Ridge, of 2 January 1985. You will not read this paper daily so the story might be new to you.

51 On 12 December 1984, a little girl called Jennifer Mangone was lying in bed. She had just fallen asleep when a wire fused in her bedroom. The crackling noise next to her bed woke her up but then she went back to sleep. An hour later she woke up again because of the smell of smoke. She knelt on her bed carefully and saw flames and smoke all around her. She screamed for her mother and loudly cried out that there was fire.

Her mother was sitting with her two-year-old daughter on her lap when she heard the child screaming. She flew up to Jennifer's room, opened the door and to her horror, saw only smoke and flames. She called to Jennifer to stay where she was and ran to the neighbours, the Leask family. She left her two-year-old daughter there and Bob Leask ran back with her.

When Bob Leask arrived at Jennifer's room he also saw only fire and smoke and he called out: "Jennifer – jump here to me. Jump!" But Jennifer, who wasn't yet nine years old, didn't dare to jump. "Jump to where you can hear my voice!" Bob called again. But Jennifer was in a panic and continued to hesitate.

Suddenly two enormous white-clad figures appeared by her shoulders. "They were too big for the house." Jennifer said later. They bent right down, picked her up by the shoulders and swung her right through the smoke and flames, straight into Bob's arms. It was about 10 feet from her bed to the door. When she looked back she could not see the angels any more.

Jennifer escaped without any symptoms of suffocation and without a single blister. In church on Sunday she moved the entire congregation to tears when she related how the angels had saved her.

In this story we again came across the curious description that the angels were 'larger' than the room. It seems that Jennifer saw two realities mixed up; the angels did not fit inside the material restrictions of the house and yet they were there.

It is that one short sentence which shows that the child's experience was a real one.

I have Jennifer's photograph in front of me. She is a

beautiful dark haired child, giving her two-year-old sister a kiss.

When angels save people's lives they are by no means always seen. In fact, I suspect that while they are present they are usually invisible and that they do their work in a quiet, modest way. If we were constantly coming across angels intervening in our lives we would never grow up. Freedom has always been one of our Heavenly Father's priorities.

52 A girl of about six had just learned to ride a bicycle and had taken a 'grown up' bike to practice riding on the street. This was at a time when there was not as much traffic as there is now. She rode along, standing on the pedals. But before she rode into the street she heard an inner voice which said: "Get off that bike!" She looked round in surprise but there was no one to be seen. The street was absolutely quiet as it often used to be before the war. Once again the voice said "Get off that bike!" And when she still didn't, the voice warned her a third time.

She got off the bike and to her utter astonishment it broke into two pieces in the street. The front fork was broken and who knows what could have happened if she had cycled on? How did she react to this? The voice no longer surprised her and she certainly didn't feel grateful. Her only concern at that moment was her anger that she could not carry the two pieces of the bicycle home by herself. It was only much later that she realized the special significance of this incident. She became a preacher.

53 The guardian angel in the following story which took place in the summer of 1989 was also invisible and yet very obviously present. The story was not written but told to me by the woman involved during a consultation. She described how she had been in the garden with her four-year-old daughter. The child was playing by the shed and she was standing some way away. The shed had a heavy glass and wire mesh door. Suddenly the mother saw to her horror that the door had come loose, perhaps because the vibrations of a passing bus had finally broken the rotting hinges, and it was falling towards the child. She was too far away to do anything about it and watched as the heavy door seemed to accelerate in slow motion as it fell on to the child. In a second her daughter would be crushed. She screamed out and the door seemed to remain suspended above the child at an angle of thirty degrees, apparently without any support. The same invisible force then snatched the child back and then the door crashed down, smashed to pieces. She was still visibly moved when she told me the story. I have known her for years and I know that she is a rational and reliable woman.

54 Another story of a girl saved by an angel took place in 1952. She was six years old at the time. She lived quite near a large rubbish tip and her parents had forbidden her to play there because it was not a safe place. They didn't tell her exactly why it was not safe. This meant that the place had a special fascination for the child. One evening, when she was walking home from her piano lesson, she decided to take the road by the rubbish tip because it was a shortcut to her home, and probably also because this would enable her to take a look at the mysterious place in a semi-permissible way.

Just next to the rubbish tip a little boy of her own age suddenly came running towards her from that direction, screaming. "Don't go that way! There's a bad man!"

But the little girl had a mind of her own, she ignored the warning and simply walked on. It was quite dark and suddenly she came face to face with a big man who looked at her threateningly and stretched his hands out towards her. She wanted to run away but felt rooted to the ground with fear. The man took a step forward and wanted to put his hands around her when she suddenly felt an enormous force behind her which seemed to suck her backwards. She was moved several meters back and kept her wits sufficiently to turn and run like the wind. This incident was still quite fresh in her mind when she wrote to me about it at the age of forty.

Someone with strong moral views might think this little girl should not have been saved. She had disobeyed her parents and patently ignored the little boy's warning. And yet she was saved, while sometimes a good child is not saved. Jesus said: "They that be whole need not a physician, but they that are sick." (Matthew 9:12). The essence of Christianity is the salvation of someone who has strayed, not the reward of goody-goodies.

To our eyes the cases of people who are saved may seem arbitrary and capricious, but one thing is certain: mercy is of supreme importance in our world. Mercy is more important than the punishment of sin.

55 One of my patients, a woman I have known for 28 years, had a similar experience to the girl on the rubbish tip, though in this case she had been a good child.

When she was 14 years old she was cycling through the dunes in Wassenaar one morning with a friend. It was still a quiet and deserted area and the two girls were enjoying the beautiful nature around them on that fine day. However, suddenly their mood changed. They sensed an unpleasant and frightening oppression.

All at once there was a man in light blue overalls standing in front of them. He had spread out his arms to tell them to stop. He had an extraordinarily beautiful face which radiated great love – the girls' fear immediately vanished. He said: "It is forbidden to go any further!" with such authority that the girls obeyed him straight away and turned back. At such a moment you don't stop to ask what the man was actually doing there. They had no idea why they had to go back but just cycled quietly back home. The next day one girl's mother asked her exactly where they had been in the dunes the day before. She had been frightened by an article in the newspaper and forbade her to go into the dunes in future. Later it appeared that at the moment they had passed the place where they had felt great fear, a psychopath had raped and murdered a twelve-year-old girl.

She did not tell her mother anything about the incident with the man but later she realized that it had not been an ordinary person who had saved her.

Why was she saved while the other girl was not? Was the angel not able to protect the other child? What are the mysteries of destiny? Again and again we come up against these unanswerable questions and have to admit to our ignorance about creation.

I believe that we do better to rejoice about those cases in which people are saved rather than grumble about the cases in which it didn't happen. From our point of view heaven is not very logical. When someone is saved this is usually an exception related to the life of the person who is saved rather than a rule which applies to every child in danger. If it were up to us we would probably have done things differently but I strongly suspect that this would really lead to problems. It is unpleasant to admit but we know too little to be capable of judging the whys and wherefores of creation.

56 Sometimes I think that angels have difficulty attracting our attention. Some years ago Marilyn Carlson from California wrote in *Guideposts* that she had spoken to a woman who had told her how she had rowed onto a lake when she was 10 years old. It was getting dark as she rowed away and before she knew it, night had fallen and it was pitch dark. The lake was very large and she had no idea where she was. Suddenly a figure like a human being appeared in the distance. He seemed to glow and was holding a lantern in his hand. He signalled to her and with all her strength the child rowed towards the spot where she could see the apparition.

At last she reached the shore but as soon as she was safely back, the figure seemed to have vanished without a trace. This is a short story of a child being saved but it is a jewel of a story. The night of this world in which we have lost our way along the path of life, and then the shining figure with a lantern standing on the shore.

It is an encounter with the light of heaven which can suddenly guide us onto the right track. It is as though this story is telling us not to be afraid in life. You may feel lost but somewhere there is dry land and a home to go back to. Heed him well, Who is in the Light!

My view that encounters with angels don't simply happen but are part of the pattern of life of the person concerned, is demonstrated by the following story. It was sent to me by a woman of eighty-five from Germany, who has died since she wrote to me. She said that this happened to the writer, Charlotte Hofmann. It is not quite clear to me where the story originated exactly. It came from an offprint of unknown origin and reveals a particular aspect of encounters with angels which is very important.

57 I will give a brief version of this story in my own words.

Just imagine a hilly, snowy landscape in Germany. There is a small town on the hillside with two roads leading down to the valley. One is a road for cars and other vehicles, the other a path through the woods. In winter you are allowed to go up with a toboggan, but not down, because there have been several accidents.

In the valley there is a large farm. A family with several children live there. The children have to help on the farm as soon as they are old enough.

The main character in this story is a twelve-year-old girl. It took place on Christmas Eve.

The farmer's wife sent her daughter with her three-year-old brother to do some last-minute shopping for Christmas in the town on the hill. She put her brother on the toboggan and took the path through the woods.

I think the child must have been rather precocious because though she was so young she was suffering a crisis of faith. She had the frightening feeling that the adults were pulling her leg, that God did not really exist at all and that the whole Christmas story was no more than a pretty fairytale. This gave her a horrible empty feeling and to make matters even worse, she was going to have to read the Christmas story in the Bible that evening.

She told herself that as they walked on she would count to a hundred to give God a chance to show her a sign. If He did not do so, He didn't exist.

I thought for a long time about whether or not to include this story but I find the idea of the child counting so convincing and so like a real child, that I could not resist it. She counted to a hundred and nothing happened. Of course, this did not resolve her dilemma, it only increased her uncertainty even futher.

She did her shopping up in the town and wanted to take the main road down. But the road had been gritted. She was tired of walking and now had the shopping as well as her little brother. Because she didn't want to drag the toboggan laboriously downhill, she decided after some hesitation, to take the forbidden path through the woods after all, and soon the two children were merrily sliding down. It was wonderful, they raced round the bends and had great fun. Then there was a sharp bend and she didn't steer the toboggan quickly enough so that they flew off the path and went straight down the slope. Unfortunately the whole slope was covered with pine trees and there was a large one right in her way. In a flash she saw what was going to happen – her brother, who was at the front would have a fractured skull and probably be killed; she might be seriously injured herself.

Then, just before they hit the tree, a man suddenly jumped in front of the toboggan. He caught it, they all capsized in the snow and came to rest, unhurt, just before the tree. The man did not say a word, did not take any notice of the girl but put the little boy back on the toboggan and took them back to the path. Then he left without a word. It was dusk and his face remained in the shadow. What was the effect on the little girl? She might have said: "That was a lucky escape! It's a good thing that man happened to be in the woods."

But this is not what she thought. This incident actually stirred the very depths of her soul. On the one hand, she was ashamed for she realized that she had almost caused a serious accident and she thought of the great sorrow of her parents if anything had happened to her brother. On the other hand, she was full of joy because she had the strong feeling that God had given her a sign that He existed after all, if not while she counted to a hundred, in His own time. She walked carefully down the mountain and that evening she was able to read the Christmas story in the Bible with her heart full of joy and her faith restored.

Was it an angel in the story? Or was it a farm worker? I have absolutely no idea. But one thing is clear: Whether an angel or a farm labourer, he gave the eleven-year-old girl the sign she needed at exactly the right time, so that she was able to strengthen her belief. Even if the man who came to her aid was not an angel, he acted as an angel.

Was this child saved because she had been particularly good? Quite the contrary, she tempted God with her counting game and that is strictly forbidden. She took the forbidden path and in this way jeopardized the life of her brother entrusted to her care.

She was only eleven years old but she knew that she had done wrong. We do not gain salvation because we are good, but because we have gone wrong. Nowadays, sin is a dirty and primitive word. A person no longer sins, he makes mistakes, for example, because he was beaten by his father as a child.

We have become so confused in the twentieth century because we have lost our sense of doing wrong. Our excuses for what we do have become so sophisticated that we can no longer see the wood for the trees.

This is why the story about this girl can teach us something important. She discovered for herself that God can redeem you just when you realize that there is no excuse for what you have been doing. The girl saw this the moment before the toboggan was going to hit the tree. The mistake she had made was totally clear to her and then she was saved.

This sort of thing is disturbing to many good people. And yet it is the message of the New Testament.

When a group of holier-than-thou priests turned up their noses in disgust that Jesus met with some people they considered to be contemptible sinners, Jesus rebuked them sharply, reminding them that he had not come to call the righteous, but the sinners (Matthew 9:13).

To summarize, it is clear that this story – as so often in stories about angels – contains two elements of mercy: saving children from mortal danger and the restoring of the girl's soul.

Our Lord has a different system of reckoning from that we use among ourselves.

After all these angel stories there is something I feel I must say. The human mind has an unfortunate habit-forming tendency. When we are children everything looks new and fresh. Colours are very bright. As we get older, creation loses some of its shine because we have got used to everything. It is only after a serious illness that the old freshness of youth may return and it seems as though colours are like we remember how they used to be. Sometimes this also happens when we see things from an unusual perspective, for example, when we see the astonishing photographs taken of the earth from a satellite. Unfortunately even miracles can become commonplace when you see too many of them. In Jerusalem I attended a healing service of Kathryn Kuhlman.

People joyfully got up from their wheelchairs, patients

suffering from cancer wept when they told how they had been cured and one moving miracle was followed by another.

Because of the tremendous interest she aroused, Kathryn held a second healing service. The strange thing was that the second evening was quite different. The same miracles were performed and yet we had more of a feeling of theatre than the first time. The number of miraculous cures was so great that they had become ordinary.

This feeling of mundanity not only affected me, but also my companion that evening. It is disgraceful to have to admit to it, but yet it is true.

I think that this is also the reason that miracles do not always change the lives of the people who have witnessed them. This was true in the days of the New Testament and still applies today. The lives of people who have been affected by a miracle themselves do usually change fundamentally. On the other hand the people who hear about these miracles all too often treat it like any other piece of news and return to the business of daily life.

This is a striking confirmation of my view that a miracle is appropriate when the recipient has reached a sort of critical charge. The button is ready to be pressed; the cocoon is at bursting point. No one is visited by an angel through pure chance or just happens to be the subject of a miracle.

A book like this is in danger of being affected in the same way as the second healing service. This danger is strikingly illustrated by Buddingh when he published his own epitaph: "Angels everywhere, but no pub to be found!" Presumably he imagines that a good pub is as difficult to find in heaven as an angel is on earth.

When there are too many angels, there is a lack of contrast. Moreover, it is very difficult to describe aspects of heaven again and again. In Dante's *Divine Comedy* the description of hell and the horrors of hell are much more fascinating than the almost abstract bliss of heaven. Why do we read exciting books? It is because all sorts of things go wrong. We would feel cheated if the hero and heroine found each other in Chapter One and the rest of the book merely described their unalloyed happiness together.

Of course, all my stories about angels are short dramas

but the deus ex machina principle is present in all the descriptions. The general pattern is that there is a person in distress and an angel comforts, advises or saves them. Then they live happily ever after except in the few cases I mentioned in which the person concerned died. This is not a bad structure for a story but I will have to change the tune a bit to keep the interest going.

This is why the next section is about encounters with angels which do not have a happy ending, from an earthly point of view.

CHILDREN AND DEATH

It seems almost presumptuous to say anything about this, when Elisabeth Kübler-Ross has written such wonderful books on the subject. With due deference to her authority, here are some of the stories from my own archives. A little boy with Dutch parents was born in South Africa. Unfortunately the little boy, who was called Arie, had a serious heart condition. When he was seven years old, his only hope of survival lay in an operation which would have to be performed in the United States. He had to be carried into the airplane. Three months later he returned, walking on his own two feet, radiant with happiness, accompanied by his parents and an unknown young doctor named Barnard. It was this doctor who subsequently astonished the whole world with the first heart transplant operation.

One day, when Arie was eight years old, he was playing on his own in the living room when his mother came in. He suddenly cried out: "Look mother, there's an angel over there!"

"I can't see anything," she answered in surprise.

"Look, over there," said the child pointing to a spot in the room and then Arie said: "Now it's gone." The next morning he was playing on the floor in another room. Again he called out the moment his mother walked into the room: "There's the angel again!" and at that moment he died.

This happened quite a long time ago. His brother and sister are now adults but no one in that family will ever forget the angel, which not only came to fetch Arie but also to comfort his parents. This comfort is also a feature of the next story which took place with Dutch people in France thirty years ago.

59 A young married couple had their first child. To their great sorrow their little boy was doubly handicapped. He would never learn to walk or talk. They loved him dearly and a few years later the woman became pregnant again. Obviously she was very worried that her next child would be handicapped as well. As her pregnancy progressed she became more and more worried. The doctor, who noticed her tension, advised her to have the handicapped son placed in a good institution for the last weeks of her pregnancy because he thought she would be more relaxed when she had the baby. She took his advice and a few weeks later she gave birth to a normal, healthy baby.

In those days the period of confinement was still 10 days. After nine days she decided to tell her doctor the next day that her oldest child could come back again, for in the past the doctor would make his last call on the tenth day and the period of confinement was over.

In the night between the ninth and tenth day she had a very strange experience. While she was wide awake she suddenly saw her handicapped son walking past her bed quite normally. He was not alone but was holding someone's hand, looking up at him and saying something. Then the other person answered.

When the doctor came to see her that morning she thought he looked tired and worried. She told him what had happened in the night, again emphasizing the fact that her paralyzed and dumb child had been walking and talking.

"Ah," said the French doctor, "the person he was walking with was his guardian angel who came to fetch him last night. I'm afraid I have to tell you that your son died in the night."

When she told the story to her husband he said: "If anyone else had told me this I would not have believed it, but you never imagine things. Now we can be sure that Rudi is happy."

I know of more examples of people who saw their handicapped child after death, with a healthy body.

It is a terrible thing when our flesh and blood no longer

wants to go on, but it is a temporary disaster. I think that the people who destroy the lives of others may be able to get round this in *this* life in a gross and powerful way, but if we could see them beyond the grave we would see that their soul was doubly handicapped.

If you are handicapped in this life, you are the victim of a difficult and dangerous world, but if you are handicapped in the next life you are your own victim.

I am convinced that every dying child is fetched by angels. Usually you do not see these angels but when they are visible this is usually to comfort the mourners, for the guardian angels of children can include one of the parents in their care.

60 In November 1962, a talented artist took her little boy up to bed. At that time she was in a state of spiritual and material crisis and was rather depressive. When she had put the child to bed, he immediately fell into a deep sleep and she lay down next to him for a while, with his warm little body close to hers. She shut her eyes and through her closed eyes suddenly saw a light, misty apparition with gold and violet colours. She quickly opened her eyes and then shut them again but the apparition remained there. But then it changed and in the middle of the cloud she saw an indescribably loving, smiling face. She was absolutely sure that she had seen her son's guardian angel and tried to reproduce what she saw then in a painting of which she sent me a photograph. This story doesn't really belong in this section but I included it here because it shows that angels are not solely concerned with the people they are protecting.

In heaven the rule seems to be that the more souls there are, the more joy.

61 The following story also clearly shows that angels not only come to fetch souls, but also come to console the people who are left behind.

A mother sent me a long and moving poem about her third son. He was born a healthy baby and prospered at first. He had his first birthday, started to walk and was a joy to the whole family. Then he became ill, though the poem does not reveal what was the matter with him.

It was Sunday morning and the boy was asleep in bed

with a high fever. His mother was downstairs listening
to a church service. The subject of the sermon was:
'Nothing happens that is not the Lord's will.' After the
sermon she went upstairs to give her sick son a drink,
but she found that he had died. She described how people
tried to console her, in a very poignant way.

"Be glad it wasn't your husband who died."

"Be glad that you had a normal child, not a handicapped
child like us."

"Luckily you're young, you can have more children."

These words did not make her feel better and the woman
felt even greater sorrow than before with this sort of
comfort. Her friends were rather like Job's friends who
tried to console him after everything that had happened
by saying that he must have been a tremendous sinner or
all those disasters would never have befallen him.

Then one night two angels came down by the side of her
bed. Her first reaction was one of shock; she was afraid
they had come to fetch her as well.

Suddenly she noticed that one of the angels was big and
the other small. She dared to look at their faces and saw
to her astonishment that the larger angel had the face of
her brother who had died at an early age while the smaller
angel had the face of her little son who had just died.
Then there was a sort of burning, flickering light which
was very gentle, completely surrounding her and the
angels. She was bathed in a heavenly light.

As a result of this experience she came to realize that there
was a meaning to life and that the threads of life are
woven into a great tapestry though the pattern remains
unknown to us. Corrie ten Boom always said: "Here, we
see only the back of the tapestry but the time will come
when we will behold the front in all its amazing beauty."
There are several things which deserve a mention about
this mother's story.

The angels with the faces of her loved ones who had died
is by no means an unfamiliar pattern in stories about
angels. I will outline below some of the beliefs which
have emerged in this respect in the course of time.

1) The idea that man has a 'heavenly twin', his spiritual
   alter ego with whom he will coalesce at the end of his
   development in an indivisible oneness. In this way our
   guardian angel is much closer to us than we imagine.

2) The idea that after death, man becomes an angel or a
devil. This concept was introduced by Swedenborg.
3) The words of Jesus in his judgement of the Sadducees
who claimed that there was no resurrection. Jesus said:
"(. . .) but (the resurrected) are as the angels of God
in heaven," (Matthew 22:30) and therefore compares
them to angels. This shows that in resurrection man
has some aspects of an angel but is not an angel
himself.

When I compare these three points to the story of this
woman I think she saw her brother and her child 'as
angels'. In a vision (the term she used herself) it was
revealed to her that she could feel sure that the child who
had died had not gone, but had returned to heaven where
he was surrounded by love.

These are my own thoughts on the subject, but I do not
claim to give a definitive answer. Our consciousness is
structured in such a way that we see everything in terms
of opposites. Perhaps the question 'angel or human' is
meaningless in the face of heaven and in that place the
relationship may have a complementary rather than a
contrasting character. In our world everything is split in
ten thousand pieces, but over there we will experience
the greatest unity behind all this variation.

I would like to make one more comment on the subject of
the sermon to which the woman was listening: "Nothing
happens that is not the will of the Lord!"

Maurice Nicoll analyzed this proposition in detail. Every
Christian is familiar with the Lord's Prayer. Those of us
who are Christians know the words: "Thy will be done
on earth as it is in heaven!" (Matthew 6:10).

We have repeated these lines so often that there is a very
real danger of saying them automatically and forgetting
the true meaning. For this reason Nicoll wrote the sentence extra clearly so that it really expressed what Jesus
wanted to teach his disciples. "Thy will *also* be done on
earth just as it is in heaven."

The inescapable conclusion of Jesus' own words is that
God's will is not usually done on earth.

The subject of the sermon: "Nothing happens on earth
that is not the Lord's will" directly contradicts the Lord's
Prayer.

All sorts of things happen on earth which are not the will of the Lord. When He gave us freedom He took the enormous risk that all sorts of things would happen against His will. Obviously it was necessary to take this risk in the plan of Creation. If it had not been taken we could never have had the free will to love God and that is the crux of the matter. The fact that God is able to weave His wonderful tapestry with the chaotic threads of our lives, is another matter. A truly great artist is always able to incorporate errors in his material so that the whole work of art gains greater depth.

Yet no one should think that all suffering, lack of concern, cruelty and mourning are God's will. It is more fruitful to see him as Someone Who is prepared to suffer with us. The Cross and His passion, His wounds, His pain and His abandonment are not things which happened only two thousand years ago. For God, everything is eternally present and we have the choice of pouring salt or balm on His wounds. He showed us that He wished to join mankind in all their suffering and death. For this reason alone it has never been difficult for me to know which religion to follow. For me there is no elevated, vaguely smiling deity who describes suffering as illusion. For me there is a suffering God who has an understanding of his creatures because He has suffered Himself.

The large amount of information which has become available about death in the second half of the twentieth century shows that many dying people see their loved ones who have died before, coming to fetch them.

A similar phenomenon can be seen in the following story.

62 The one-month-old baby of a married couple died in August 1945. In 1983, the woman who had lost her baby was lying awake one night and suddenly saw a small child standing at the foot of her bed one summer's night, looking not at her, but at her husband. Her husband slept quietly. She had only one thought in her mind: "That is our child from heaven and he has come to fetch his father." She switched on the light and was no longer able to see the child, but when she switched off the light again, she saw that he was still there.

However, this time he looked at her.

She was frightened by this incident and thought that she

would lose her husband. There was actually no reason
for this as he was in good health. Nevertheless, she had
interpreted the incident correctly for he died six months
later.

Again it is striking that this creature from another world
stood at the foot of the bed, the place reserved for the
guardian angel. Can a guardian angel in some cases mean
death? There is another singular aspect to this story.

Her baby had died thirty-nine years before. Why did she
think the child was their child? This poses a very difficult
question. Do children who die at an early age, grow up
in heaven? Do they grow more slowly than on earth?

Should we see the whole experience in a much more
symbolic light and remember that a child which has died
always remains a child to its mother, as long as she lives?
Was the woman mistaken about the identity of the apparition from heaven? I certainly cannot answer any of these
questions. They enter the mind but then remain unresolved.

If there are no clear revelations in this respect, it is obviously not meant for us to know.

After receiving the Torah, Israel said: "The secret things
belong unto the Lord our God: but those things which
are revealed belong to us and to our children for ever,
that we may do all the words of this law." (Deuteronomy
29:29).

This is a sobering verse for people living in a century
when all secrets must be known, whatever the cost.

CHRISTMAS ANGELS

This book would not be complete without a few real
Christmas angels.

The following story took place in Lethbridge, Alta,
America. The reader may wonder wherever I found this
story. No one gets very far without a bit of luck and I
owe my good fortune to the following events. Many
years ago I used to have an old lady in my practice who
was suffering from cancer. Through her I came into contact with an old friend of hers whom she had met in
Berlin when her husband was there before the war. This
old friend was Swiss, and when he was working he had

been a famous cancer therapist who had saved many people's lives with his unorthodox methods. Meanwhile, he had moved to California and when he was visiting Europe I met him at my patient's home. On that occasion we only talked about alternative methods of treating cancer but since then this old colleague has sent me several large envelopes. They always contain a colourful collection of cases relating to two different fields: medicine and miracles. Although I never told him, he sensed my interest in matters which are not rational, and every few months I still receive a fat envelope from my old friend. One of these contained the following newspaper article, probably from a local newspaper.

63 The journalist, Milton Atwater, began the article by describing Sara Holbrook, aged nine, decorating the Christmas tree, together with her mother Cissy and her father Gale.

The family had all been in bed for quite a while when Sara remembered that she had forgotten to put the Christmas angel on the top of the tree. She felt so strongly that the job was unfinished that she got out of bed and went to the living room. She found the aluminium angel and managed to place it on the top of the tree. Then something very strange happened. The angel started talking to her. She couldn't see him talking because it was in her head but she heard: "Be careful, there is something wrong with the wiring of the candles. If you don't do anything about it, the whole house will burn down." Sara was afraid and said later: "I didn't know that things which are not alive can still speak!" She ran to her parents, woke them up and told them what she had heard. Gale and Cissy thought that Sara had been dreaming, but to be on the safe side they took the electric plug of the Christmas tree candles out of its socket. (Americans quite happily leave their Christmas tree lit up all night.)

The next day they asked Cissy's brother who was an electrician, to check the wiring. He found that some of the wiring was so dangerous that the Christmas tree was like a time bomb. "If the lights had been left on fifteen minutes longer the whole house would have burnt down!" he said. "I just don't understand how a piece of aluminium could have told Sara that," Cissy said later.

Thinking about it, it is clear that Sara projected the warning voice which she heard within herself onto the aluminium angel. Older people may remember the endearing creation of Fernandel in which he played the rather headstrong village priest, Don Camillo. The priest had long disputes with the little statue of Christ in his church. He actually projected his inner voice onto this statue and this led to the amusing situation in which Don Camillo said what he wished to do (in his own voice) while the statue changed his mind for him in a friendly but decisive way (in a deeper, quieter voice).

Children are surprisingly close to angels. You see this clearly in their eyes. Just listen to the next story.

64 An eighty-five-year-old woman from Germany wrote to me about an extraordinary experience she had had when she was five years old. It was almost Christmas and the Christmas tree was in the room but she was not allowed to go into the room or even look into it because it was still a surprise. However, when she walked past the room she noticed that the door was open and she carefully looked round the corner. There was the Christmas tree decked out in all its glory and all the candles were on the tree. They were real candles for in 1901, when this story took place, there were no electric candles yet.

However, she saw even more. In front of the Christmas tree there was an enormous angel wearing a draped white robe and with beautiful wings spread out, lighting the candles. The child looked on, fascinated but she suddenly realized that she wasn't allowed to be there and quickly walked away. The strange thing is that the old lady still has a crystal clear memory of this event.

With regard to this story, Charles Dickens' *A Christmas Carol* springs to mind, in which the spirit of Christmas Present shows Scrooge round. The spirit, a giant who has been roused, is dressed in a dark green cloak, trimmed with white fur and clasped with a golden belt. He is holding a large torch in his hand, passing around invisible blessings and friendly words everywhere. He only has to sprinkle some of the frankincense from his torch onto people to put them into a good Christmas mood.

I think that the family of this five-year-old girl was a

good and happy family and that the clairvoyance which many little children have, enabled her to perceive an angel guarding over their house who had lit the light even before the humans could do so literally, with a match.

ANGELS IN DIFFERENT SITUATIONS

People who have read my first book will remember that I referred to higher hierarchies of angels such as archangels, cherubim, etc. You may wonder if anyone has written to me about these higher angels. In fact a few people have, although these are exceptional cases. I will start with part of a very moving letter which I received from someone in Germany. It was a long letter and I will only repeat here what is relevant to this book.

65 The woman concerned told me how she had grown up in a hard environment without love. She describes her parents as cruel, heartless people who were utterly selfish and lived only for their own pleasure although they appeared very jolly to the outside world. At every available opportunity they told her they had not wanted her and that they couldn't understand how fate had dealt them this blow despite several attempts to perform an abortion.

They did not take any notice of her and left servants to bring her up. They were wealthy; her father was a diplomat.

In her whole life her mother never once stroked her hair, comforted or helped her, and the icy atmosphere in the family home was unbearable to this sensitive, warm-hearted child. She was constantly beaten for no reason. She could only speak when someone asked her a question and when she answered, they would shout: "You're lying."

The child's background seems to have come straight from the spine-chilling book *People of the Lie*, by the American psychiatrist, M. Scott Peck. In this book he states that in addition to people who are disturbed so that they are not fully accountable for their evil deeds, there are also people who are simply evil.

They know exactly what they are doing but they just go on doing it. Peck says that he feels the chill of fear run down his back when he meets such people. This sort of person is often found in privileged backgrounds. They are prosperous and outwardly eminently respectable, but woe betide anyone who is closely involved with such a person.

When she was only five years old the girl in this story was so desperate that one day, when her parents were out, she went to look for a priest and asked him to help her end her life. The good man was dismayed and told her about angels who were always ready to help. The girl's background was not religious and as she did not know what to make of a great omnipotent God or of Jesus Christ, she began to pray fervently to the angels, begging them to help her.

It was almost her sixth birthday, a day like any other because no one paid any attention to it.

One night she suddenly woke up because someone was pulling her out of bed and then put her down at the little writing desk in her bedroom. She sat there shivering with cold and fear.

However, all of a sudden there was a gigantic figure standing next to her, completely dressed in linen garments and so large that the upper part of his body passed through the ceiling of her room reaching up to the ceiling of the top floor. Curiously, she could see this very well. Then the figure gave her some drawing implements, took her hand and slowly and carefully drew a head surrounded by blue feathers. When the drawing was finished she said: "That is an angel. Is that you?" "Yes," he said. "What is your name?" she asked. "Michael," he replied. He had a deep, almost metallic voice which was penetrating but not dominating like her father's voice. Then the figure slowly dissolved. Although no one noticed, she experienced a profound inner development from that time on, but she never talked to anyone else about this and her other encounters with angels.

I would like to mention another event from her life. She was eleven years old when a very sad event took place. Her grandfather, who lived with them and whom she loved dearly, died. Her father insisted that he should lie in state in the hall until the funeral. When the little girl went to the toilet in the night she had to pass through the hall. This filled her with such panic that she wet her bed. The servants told her parents straightaway. They gave her a beating but that was not all. In the evening she was placed in the hall with her back to the coffin, her bottom bare and left there until dawn.

When she was standing there in the middle of the night, cold and miserable, she heard a deep voice which said: "Turn around, do not be afraid!" She turned round and it looked as though a soft bluish light was radiating from the feet of her dead grandfather. She was held by the shoulders and gently moved to the head of the coffin. There she saw the light becoming stronger and acquiring an increasingly definite shape. Finally there was an enormous shining figure, dressed in a golden yellow robe, standing in front of her. He was as tall as the ceiling far above her. He had bare feet and his clothes, though not transparent, seemed ethereal.

He said a few things to her and made some movements over her grandfather's body. She thought she heard her grandfather's voice saying: "Raphael."

At this point I would just like to add that later in her life she forgave everyone who had treated her cruelly and that she was a blessing to many people. Outwardly her childhood was a torment, but she had a shining inner soul which developed despite all the oppression.

Just as there were children in some of the stories in the other chapters, I will also include some adults in this chapter about children. This is in connection with higher angels.

66 A young woman was seated at the organ in a village church in Northern Germany. Something happened to her which she finds impossible to describe in words. It was so overwhelming that it was thirty years before she wrote the following poem:

"I saw him
Cast in ore,
surrounded by light, a green light
with eyes, hundreds of eyes and more hundreds of eyes,
behind me,
and I was filled with fear.

"I saw him
Cast in ore,

A sword resting in his hands, strong.
With eyes, hundreds of eyes and more hundreds of eyes
behind me,
and I was filled with fear."

I wrote to her to ask her to explain these enigmatic words
and she told me that, as she was seated at the organ, she
was suddenly changed. The only way she could express
it was to say that she had become all eye. She could look
in every direction, even behind her, and high above the
ground, through one of the church windows behind her,
she saw a figure standing in the sky. He had a sword in
his hand pointing downwards like a cross. I can only
explain this as an experience of a cherubim, which has
been described as a creature full of eyes within and all
around (Ezekiel and The Gospel According to St John).
However, the woman assured me that it had been she
herself who was full of eyes.
It seems possible that the proximity of such a high angel
could overwhelm someone so completely that there is a
sort of temporary coalescence of the angel and the person
so that for a while that person sees what the angel per-
ceives. The experience shocked the woman so profoundly
that she kept it to herself for thirty years until she finally
wrote down the poem quoted above in translation, in
1985. She also set the poem to music and was at last able
to integrate the incident in her life and think about it
without fear.

67 Another story about a higher angel comes from a
Jewish woman who experienced many hardships
in the war. After the war she became a nurse and went
to the tropics. In the hospital where she worked there
was discrimination against the coloured people and
because she had personally experienced what this meant,
she constantly stood up for these people to the extreme
irritation of the hospital staff.
One day she was hauled on the mat yet again, but this
time they had her. There were nine men behind the table,
led by the inspector of health. He began to read out a
letter which contained an unjust accusation against her,
relating to a serious error. She was absolutely sure that
she had never been guilty of this error but they obviously

intended to dismiss her from her post on the basis of the unjust accusation. As she stood there, feeling very unhappy, the Archangel Gabriel appeared to her and flew up with her in his tremendous wings. When she came to herself in the room she felt as though she had been away for hours and she just caught the inspector of health's words: "You can go, but let this be a warning to you." She was filled with an intense feeling of bliss and this lasted for many weeks. The strange thing was that all the people who had falsely accused her fell ill in the next few years. She still experiences her life as a single long miracle. I will not end these stories by asking if they are true or not true.

If I had not been convinced that these people had really experienced these things I would not have included the stories in the book.

After these rather overwhelming angels it is necessary to slow down a bit and relate a story which could be described as the soft beating of wings.

68 A thirteen-year-old Dutch girl was touring the Haute Savoie with her mother and fifteen-year-old sister. They were walking high up in the mountains and were on the point of going down in a cable car. A few minutes before she said to her mother: "I just have to go to the toilet." When she came back she noticed that the cable car had just left. Her mother was not at all cross and said: "Never mind, we'll just take the next one." A bit later there was a tremendous shuddering noise. The cable car had come off its rails on a bend and crashed down onto the road many metres below. The three of them went down on foot to the place of the accident, a terrible experience. Were these the wings of a guardian angel? Was it a lucky coincidence? Or is a lucky coincidence the same thing as the wings of an angel?

The next story is about a wicked thought which suddenly comes to a nice child.

69 Just imagine a German village. A group of children plays in the village every afternoon like anywhere else in the world. There is a ten-year-old boy in the group. He is the weakest of all of them. When a ball is thrown, he misses it, he never wins a game of What's the time Mr Wolf? and is always the first to be found when they play hide and seek. He constantly has to be on his toes to join in with the others.

Apart from the games that all children play, this group also did much more dangerous things. They played wild, adventurous games in which they were armed with bows and arrows. Not one of these harmless little bows and arrows which couldn't harm a fly, but real hunting bows and arrows with a considerable range, with the arrow penetrating deeply. The bows and arrows were a real status symbol for the children of this group. They shot at old boxes and discs and the sharp arrows pierced them and had to be ripped out again with some force.

It is well known that the weakest and slowest member of a group of children has a very hard time. He is the target for all the bullies among the boys and this also applied for the ten-year-old lad, whom I shall call Siegfried for the present purposes. One day, when the boys were walking through the woods, obviously armed with their bows and arrows, he was being taunted once again by the bigger, stronger boys. At a certain point little Siegfried could take no more of the tormenting and flung himself at one of the bigger boys in a terrible rage. However, this boy just walked away laughing at him, and because he was faster Siegfried could not catch him up. The he fitted an arrow in the bow, drew it back as far as it would go and aimed between the shoulder blades of the boy who was running away. He shot the arrow and it whistled straight towards the target. Just at the moment that the arrow left the bow he became aware of how dangerous it was and how thoughtless he had been.

The arrow had almost reached the boy and Siegfried stood rooted to the ground watching as the arrow seemed to be taken by an invisible hand just before hitting its target, flying up almost perpendicularly straight over the head of the unsuspecting boy who was still running away into the woods.

Siegfried was very relieved and that afternoon he played with the group as usual. No one had seen anything.

The peculiar thing is that it was several years before he started thinking about the strange thing that had happened. When he wrote to me at the age of 25 he was convinced that his guardian angel had deflected the arrow from its trajectory to prevent him from seriously wounding or possibly even killing another child.

The only thing I would like to point out in connection with this story is Siegfried's clear awareness of what he had done wrong just before a higher power intervened. I believe this is of essential importance. It was precisely because of his clear awareness that the incident was permanently engraved on his mind, and was able to exert a healing influence on the rest of Siegfried's life.

Is this a true story? I believe it is. I think it is a wonderful story and for me one of the aspects which lend it credibility is that it was many years before Siegfried thought that it was a very strange and even impossible thing to happen. This corresponds entirely with the way in which children in their semi-magical way of thinking accept the most improbable things as being normal.

70 Finally, to conclude this section, here is a story about a child on the brink of puberty. It was sent to me by a woman who was 65 when she wrote to me. It concerned something which had happened to her in 1934 when she was thirteen years old.

She had to take the train from O, where she lived, to school in S every day. One day her mother gave her a parcel and said: "Remember, this is very important. When you finish school today, get off at Sulzbuck and give this parcel to your aunt. It is a very important parcel, so take good care of it."

When she looked on her desk at the end of the last lesson that afternoon, the parcel had disappeared without trace. She realized straightaway that she had left it on the train on the way to school that morning.

She was distraught and went in tears to her teacher, a kindly nun, to tell her what had happened.

"Come" she said. "Let us pray together." So they did.

When she arrived at the station half an hour later than usual, the train had gone. However, the next train was already there and she got in.

It was a long carriage with many empty seats because no one, apart from herself, had got in yet. She sat by the door and her tears ran quietly down her cheeks.

Suddenly a voice from the other end of the carriage said: "Why are you crying?" She said: "I left a very important parcel on the train this morning." She looked up through her tears and saw a boy of her own age standing in front of her.

"Look up, you will see your parcel," he said.

And it was true, the parcel was on the wooden luggage shelf above her head. She didn't understand how this was possible but took it down from the shelf overjoyed. Happy and astonished she wanted to thank the boy but he had completely vanished.

Do angels concern themselves with lost parcels? I think the concept 'important' and 'unimportant' are different in heaven and on earth. When you look at the incredible sophistication of the microscopic world you realize that big and small do not exist in Creation. Infinite care has been devoted to every detail.

Perhaps all our little events are very important for heaven and the thing to which we attribute such importance are merely a shrug of the shoulders in heaven.

CHAPTER 5

ANGELS AND
WAR

This chapter consists of two parts.
The first deals with the influence of heaven in war
and events during war.
The second contains eyewitness accounts of people who
have been helped by angels in events during a war.

ANGELS AND THE TURMOIL OF WAR

The first story is set in Holland and is not about the
intervention of an angel but about a prophecy by an
angel. Thus this is an example of the angel's traditional
role as a messenger. E. Smit recorded the story for pos-
terity and published it in 1965 in *Een Nieuw Geluid* (A
New Sound). He took the story from a book which was
published in 1704, Zedelijke en stichtelijke gezangen
(Moral and Devotional Songs) by Jan Luijken.

71 1672 was a year of disaster for the Netherlands. Jan
    and Cornelis de Witt were governing the country
together as regents. It was a time when there were no
vice-regents. The De Witt brothers did all they could to
maintain the peace with their neighbouring countries but
in that year the republic was unexpectedly attacked by
England, France, Munster and Cologne.
The history of the Netherlands chronicles this period as

a time when the government was in despair, the country without hope and the people without reason.

The following incident occurred in that year.

A virtuous widow by the name of Grietje Klaas lived in Zaandam, on the west side of the Kattegat. When war broke out she was very worried, with good reason. Holland had maintained its fleet very well but the army was weak, and strong well-trained armies were marching into Holland.

I will write down the account as it was written at that time by Jan Luijken, to give an indication of the style.

Thus, on 14 April, that being the day before Easter Sunday, she went to bed in a melancholy humour at about half past nine in the evening, leaning her elbow on the bed with her hand behind her head, with the shutters of the windows closed. While she was thus seated a great light filled the room, in which was revealed an Angel, appearing as a beautiful youth, standing about eight or 10 feet from the bed (opposite her) and slightly bowing his head to the right. He looked upon her with great love and her heart rejoiced so that she said that she was well content and wished no greater joy in heaven. His gown was white and long, reaching to his feet. His appearance was wonderful and he was of great size, as tall as the full reach of a man of average size. His wings were as high as his head, the feathers pointing down, not spread out in flight. On his head he wore a sort of leather cap which was white. The sides of his head were covered with curly hair. Through his left elbow there were long feathers, the plume pointing up and reaching above his head. The feather was of a light grey colour at the end. From his left fore-arm there was a small chestnut coloured twig, a yard long, with small tips, each an inch long which were turning green at the ends. With his arms spread out he bent them round so that his hands met.

Thus, when he bent his arms round, a voice spoke loud and clear (although she could not distinguish what manner of voice it was, whether the external voice or the inner voice of the soul): "Thus shall God preserve Holland."

Then she thought: We are within Holland, we shall be preserved. According to his testimony this beauteous vision remained there for half an hour rather than a quarter of an hour. The figure of the Angel appeared to be of silver from top to bottom. The voice spoke a second time: "The Angel of the Lord encampeth round about them that fear him," and she thought: "Those words are taken from psalm 34."

Then this face disappeared and Grietje Klaas wished to conceal what had happened. She was very afraid until she revealed this event to someone and then she was relieved. Afterwards she spoke freely to all people, for The Glory of God.

This took place and was known to many people, even to hundreds of people, before it was known what things would come to pass. Yea, as everyone knows, it all happened quite the contrary to what was expected. It is a mystery to all reasonable people. The good God preserved Holland in his fatherly arms in a singular fashion without the assistance of any persons. We heard this from her own lips while she lived.

It is quite true that everything was unexpectedly resolved in this period of the history of Holland.

On the occasion of these events, Jan Luijken wrote a poem. I would like to include a fragment of this work.

'A great Herald, in white apparel
Where did he appear? To great cities did he travel?
To the Prince's court or is it that he came
To a scholarly Doctor of great fame?
Oh no, but as is told to all
God's will chooses all things small.
Quite different from how the world remarks
Is God, and all that His great wisdom works
It was in a village, a cottage which lies
In a humble place, which the great despise,
That a woman saw, forgotten but upright
The divine servant, in the Divine light,
Praise be to God, and the love that He doth give
To show that all around us He doth live.'

This story has some striking similarities to some of the modern stories about angels. The preference for the bedroom. The bright light shining in the room, the simple background of the witness.

Obviously the branch and the feather had a symbolic

significance. In those days the feather was used for writing: it was pointing down and was grey at the top.

I see this as a symbol of the De Witt brothers whose time was past. In the sprouting twig I see the coming of Stadholder Willem III who took over the government not long afterwards. Later he became King of England. This is my personal interpretation for there is no reference to this in the original document.

We will now leave the seventeenth century and move on to the eighteenth century.

72 This is a famous story about angels dating from the time that America was gaining its liberation from England.

The main character in this story is George Washington. He was born in the United States on 22 February 1732 and was the founder of the independence of a nation which would become the most powerful nation in the world. As the general of the American forces he eventually defeated the English army vainly trying to retain the English colony, in a war which progressed with many ups and downs. At the end of the war he was elected to become the first president of the United States.

Probably few people in Europe are aware that during the War of Independence Washington had an important experience involving an angel. He told two of the officers on his staff about this experience. One of these was Anthony Sherman, who was eighteen years old at the time. He kept Washington's confidence to himself all his life, without telling anyone about it. One day when he was ninety-nine years old he was standing in front of the Independence Hall with his friend Wesley Bradshaw. The building strongly reminded him of the War of Independence in which he had fought himself. His eyes started to shine and he asked his friend to walk into the Hall with him. Then he said: "I would like to tell you about an event in Washington's life which no one else knows about. Note well the predictions which I will pass on to you for you will see them fulfilled in your own lifetime."

Fortunately Sherman's mind was still very lucid and he recounted the tale below. This was on the 4th of July 1859 and he died shortly afterwards. That same year his story was published. In 1931, the editors of the magazine

Destiny discovered it and since then the magazine has published it several times, and every time the issue containing the story sells out immediately. Although it concerns a very detailed experience I have nevertheless included it in full and included it here because it is a unique document. Sherman told the following story: 'From the beginning of the revolution we passed through all the vicissitudes of fate, sometimes good, sometimes bad, occasionally victorious and then defeated. I think the darkest period was when Washington retreated to Valley Forge where he decided to spend the winter of 1777 after several defeats.

'Oh, I often saw tears running down the care-worn cheeks of our dear old commander when he talked about the conditions of his poor soldiers, to an officer who was in his confidence. No doubt you have heard the story of how Washington went into the bushes to pray. Not only was that true, but he often prayed in secret for the assistance and comfort of God, whose divine mediating powers took us safely through those dark days of our trials.

'One day – I remember it well – when the bitterly cold wind was whistling through the leafless trees, and the sun shone brightly in a cloudless sky, he stayed in his room on his own all afternoon. When he came outside I noticed that his face was paler than usual, his soul seemed to be full of something of extraordinary importance. Dusk was falling when he sent a servant to the rooms of the officer of the guard with a request to come to him. When he arrived we talked for about half an hour and then Washington said to us: "I do not know whether it is because of my anxiety or something else but this afternoon, as I was sitting at my table writing an urgent report there was something in the room that disturbed me. I looked up and saw an extremely beautiful woman standing opposite me. Because I had given strict orders that I was not to be disturbed I was so surprised that it was a while before I could utter a word to ask her why she was there. I repeated my question a second, third and even fourth time but my mysterious guest gave no answer, except to slightly raise her eyes. At the same time a strange feeling made it impossible for me to do anything. Once again I tried to speak to her but I had lost my tongue, even my mind was paralyzed. A new influence, mysterious, powerful, irresistible, took possession of me. The only thing I could do was to stare at my unknown visitor steadily, without moving.

'"Gradually it seemed as though the atmosphere was filled with strange vibrations and became luminous. Everything around me seemed to become more ethereal and the mysterious visitor herself became more airy and yet more distinct to my eyes than before. I began to feel like someone who is dying, or rather I had sensations which I sometimes imagine are like those which accompany death. I did not think, I was only conscious of staring fixedly and mindlessly at my guest.

'"Then I heard a voice say: 'Son of the Republic, look and learn!'

'"At the same time my visitor stretched out her arm to the east. I saw a heavy white vapour swirling and rising up at a distance. The mist gradually cleared and I looked upon a strange scene. In front of me all the countries of the world were stretched out: Europe, Asia, Africa, America. I saw the waters of the Atlantic Ocean rolling in between Europe and America, and between Asia and America. I saw the movement of the Pacific Ocean. Then the same mysterious voice repeated: 'Son of the Republic, look and learn!' After that moment I saw a dark shadowy figure like an angel standing or rather floating in the middle of the air between Europe and America. He scooped some water from the ocean and sprinkled some of it on America with his right hand, and on Europe with his left hand. Immediately dark clouds rose up from those lands, joining together over the middle of the ocean. The cloud formed in this way hung for a while and then slowly moved to the west until it encompassed America with its dark fields. Vivid flashes of lightning shot intermittently through the clouds and I heard the suppressed cries and groans of the American people. A second time the angel scooped water from the ocean and sprinkled it like the first time. The dark cloud was then drawn back to the ocean and disappeared in the lapping waves. A third time I heard the mysterious voice say: 'Son of the Republic, look and learn!'

'"I turned my gaze to America and saw villages and

towns and cities appearing one by one until they were
scattered over the entire country from the Atlantic Ocean
to the Pacific Ocean.

'"Then the dark, shadowy angel turned his face to the
south and I saw an ominous ghost approaching our
country from Africa. He glided slowly and heavily over
every town and city and then the inhabitants prepared for
battle against each other. As I looked I saw a shining
angel bearing a crown of light with the word 'Union'.
He carried the American flag which he placed between
the people of the divided nation and said: 'Remember
that you are brothers.' Immediately the inhabitants threw
down their arms and made friends, united under the
national banner.

'"Once again I heard the mysterious voice saying: 'Son
of the Republic, look and learn!' Then the dark, shadowy
angel put a trumpet to his mouth and sounded three clean
notes and when he had taken water from the ocean he
sprinkled it on Europe, Asia and Africa. Then my eyes
beheld a terrible scene. From each of these continents rose
thick black clouds which soon massed together. A dark
red light glowed through these towering clouds. By this
light I saw hordes of armed men, moving with the cloud,
marching over land, and sailing over the sea to America,
while the land was completely covered with cloud.
Vaguely, I saw these enormous armies destroy the entire
country and burn the villages, towns and cities which I
had seen arise. As I listened to the thunder of the cannon,
the clashing of the swords and the screams and cries of
millions of people embroiled in mortal combat, I once
again heard the mysterious voice say: 'Son of the Republic, look and learn!'

'"Then the voice was silent, the dark shadowy angel
again put the trumpet to his lips and sounded a long and
fearful call. Immediately a light as of a thousand stars
shone down upon me from above, penetrating the dark
cloud which enveloped America so that it broke up completely. At the same time the angel on whose head the
word 'Union' still glittered, descended from heaven holding our national flag in one hand and a sword in the other
hand and accompanied by legions of shining figures.
These immediately joined the ranks of the inhabitants of
America who had almost reached the depths of despair

but now took courage straightaway, reforming their broken lines and renewing their battle. I heard the mysterious voice say: 'Son of the Republic, look and learn!' When the voice stopped speaking I saw the shadowy angel scoop water from the ocean and sprinkle it on America for the last time. Immediately the dark cloud rolled back together with the armies which it had brought with it, leaving the inhabitants of the land victorious. Again I saw how villages, towns and cities arose where they had formerly been, while the shining angel planted the banner he had brought with him among them and called out in a loud voice: 'As long as the stars continue to exist and the dew falls on earth from heaven, the republic will go on.' He took the crown from his head with the word 'Union' flashing on it and placed it on the banner, while the people knelt down and said 'Amen'.

Straightaway the scene started to blur and dissolve and finally I saw only the swirling mist rising up as I had seen in the beginning. When this also disappeared I once again gazed upon the mysterious visitor who said in the same voice I had heard at first: 'Son of the Republic, what you have seen is explained as follows: The Republic will suffer three great disasters. The most terrible is the second of these and when it is past the whole of the world together will not be able to triumph over it. Let every child of the Republic learn to live for his God, his country and the Union.' With these words he vanished and I stood up from my chair and felt that I had seen a vision which showed me the birth, the progress and the destiny of the United States."

'My distinguished companion concluded: "These were the words of Washington, which I heard from his own mouth, and America would do well to take heed of them."'

Tremendous, such an old man who walks round all his life with a pearl of wisdom, to pass it on just before the end of his life. In this way I have received jewels of stories from old people who managed to tell them just before they died. George Washington's experience was a sort of apocalypse. There is a striking similarity with the Revelations of St John which describes the three woes (Revelations 8:13), also heralded by angels blowing a trumpet.

It is not very difficult to identify the first and second disaster in Washington's story. The first was the war against England and he was still in the middle of this. The second was the very bloody American Civil War which was primarily about the abolition of slavery. The appearance of the ghost from Africa probably refers to the negro slave trade which caused such bitter conflict in America. In Europe we know very little about the Civil War, although we have learnt something about it from a number of television serials. Hundreds and thousands of people fell in that conflict. The third part of the prophecy is still the future. America is now so powerful that it is impossible to imagine the country being invaded, but situations can change so rapidly – as Sherman said – that we would be well advised to heed the warning.

We would consider the last disaster to be the worst but the angel thought differently. She thinks civil war is worse than invasion, perhaps because the former involves brothers fighting brothers. In this context I am reminded of one of Shakespeare's plays in which two armies are fighting each other on English soil and a father on the battle field realizes to his horror that he has just killed his son who was fighting on the other side, while a little later a son is utterly dismayed to find he has killed his father (King Henry VI, part 3, act 2, scene V).

We will now take a leap forward in history into our own century.

In my last book I told the story of the white cavalry of Ypres in which an army of angels prevented the Germans from breaking through the British lines. This story led to some furious remarks from a German gentleman. He checked the story himself and had come to the conclusion that there had been no battle at Ypres and that the story about this battle was no more than allied propaganda. It is a very extraordinary 'coincidence' that I received a letter from an intelligent German woman who wrote to me as follows:

"In the First World War my father was a soldier in the German trenches near Ypres. For months on end they stood waist high in water which came from the flooded land. I can only confirm the strange incident involving an army of angels." She went on to say that for a while all the soldiers had been blind, though no one knew why this had happened. Their eyes were not damaged and later they all regained their sight. During the Second World War this woman was with the intelligence branch of the German Luftwaffe and she is therefore someone who gives a great deal of thought to what she writes down.

Thus the angry man who even accused me of sinning against the Holy Ghost was out of luck. He should not think that I am portraying the Lord as a biased judge. I have no idea whether He is impartial or not, but I do know that the whole of the Old Testament is one long story about God's intervention in the history of mankind. He did not abandon the world and leave it to its own devices. From time to time He intervenes because this is apparently necessary for the course of history.

We were given our freedom to make of it what we could, but occasionally we are put on the right track. Why this way and not another way, I do not know. Sometimes you have a suspicion but that is all. The white cavalry of Ypres was not the first incident of its kind in the First World War. In 1914 the following events took place.

73 At the end of August there was a battle between the British and German armies near the city of Mons. After sweeping aside all resistance, the Germans had marched straight into the heart of Belgium, maintaining a broad front. Although the Belgians, French and British stoutly defended themselves, the most severe attacks were on the British. Their troops were very much in the minority and had already fought continuously for several days with very little rest. The men were almost falling over with exhaustion. The had fought lengthy rearguard battles in which they had suffered heavy casualties and lost many cannons. A terrible defeat seemed inevitable, particularly as they had hardly any reserves left. The men realized that they were facing a day of great endurance and that only God could help them. The churches were full and the whole of the British nation prayed. Then an event took place which was subsequently known as the appearance of the 'Angels of Mons' and which was seen by many people as an answer to the fervent national prayer. The following two versions of the many descriptions of the appearance of the angels are typical. Both were told by British soldiers who

swore that they spoke from personal experience. While
a division of British soldiers was withdrawing straight
through the city of Mons under heavy German artillery
and machine gun fire in August 1914, they hastily erected
a barricade to try and slow down the enemy invasion.
There was intense fire on both sides and the air shook
with the deafening thunder of exploding hand grenades.
Suddenly, the firing stopped on both sides and there was
a deathly silence. When the British soldiers looked over
their barricades they saw four or five wonderful creatures, much larger than people, standing between them
and the silenced Germans. They were dressed in white,
bareheaded and seemed to be floating rather than standing. Their backs were to the British and they faced the
Germans, their arms and their hands stretched out as
though they were saying: "Stop! Here, and no further!"
The sun was shining very brightly. The next thing the
British saw was the Germans retreating in a very dis-
orderly fashion.

Here is another story (or is it a different version of the
same story or an analogous story?).

74 The British were almost surrounded by the Germans. They had suffered heavy losses, but it was
just when things seemed hopelessly lost that the enemy
fire suddenly ceased and a great silence fell. The heavens
opened with a bright light and shining figures appeared.
They seemed to float between the British and Allied
forces and prevented the Germans from advancing. Some
of the units of the German cavalry tried to advance despite
this, but the officers and men were unable to make the
horses move forward. Before the astonished British
troops realized what was happening, the apparently victorious German troops were retreating in chaos. This
enabled the British and allied forces to regroup and retreat
to a defence line several miles to the west where they dug
trenches. This was followed by a period of trench warfare
which lasted for three years until the spring of 1918, with
fluctuating successes on both sides. Like the story of the
white cavalry, these stories were recorded by Captain
Cecil Lightwick, a staff officer of the first corps of the
British Intelligence Service. ★(see page 190)
Were these 'angels by the motorway' stories? In England

there is still a great deal of controversy on this subject. However, it is worth noting how much the intervention described in the last story resembles the intervention predicted to George Washington – with regard to the third trial to face the United States in the future (which is still in the future at this moment in time).

Is it true or is it a case of 'monkey roll' – that is the question regarding these stories about the angels of Mons, and we would probably tend to include them in the 'monkey roll' category if they were the only ones of their kind. However, this is not the case. Those who have read my book *Angels as the Guardians and Helpers of Mankind* will remember a story I included which I had heard from my geography teacher in 1940. It concerned the saving of the Finnish army which was surrounded by the Russians. He related how an enormous angel had acted as a saviour, and at the end of the story I wrote: "Perhaps it is only a good story, which arose from the needs of the times. I have never spoken to a Finn who saw the angel." Because of the absence of an eyewitness I hesitated to publish the story about the Finnish angel, but there was another reason for my hesitation. I had heard it when I was 14. Was my memory sufficiently reliable? It is difficult to describe my joy when I received four letters about the Finnish angel after the book was published. Unfortunately there was still no eyewitness but the stories indicate so strongly that there was an angel that I still hope to speak to an eye witness at some time. Here are the summaries of the letters I received.

75 1. A German woman wrote to me that she had heard a lecture by Professor Willenius from Helsinki, who wondered how such a small country as Finland had been able to defend itself against such a great power as Russia. Then he read out a newspaper article compiled by journalists who had collected information about the appearance of the angel from all sorts of leading figures after the Finnish-Russian war. This resulted in the following story: it was 24 December 1939. For many days there had been heavy fire on both sides. It was impossible to get supplies to the front line of the Finnish army because everything that moved was mown down. Ammunition was

scarce, the hide-outs could not be repaired, all in all it was a hopeless situation. The Finns decided to fight to the last bullet and the last man, because they preferred to die rather than surrender their fatherland. As night fell the fighting had become even more severe with heavy fire on both sides. At about midnight on the night of 24 to 25 December it was suddenly so bright that their eyes were blinded. The shooting stopped and when the soldiers' eyes had accustomed slightly to the brightness they were able to distinguish a large angel who was holding a luminous cross in his hand which was pointing to Finland. That night it was possible to get supplies to the front line and that is how the Finns won the war.

2. In 1986 I received a letter from a woman in Helsinki who had read my book. She wrote: "It is no fairytale that the angel was seen. We all know about it here. Please write to the General Staff for they can confirm the story. It was reported in the newspapers in 1940. She enclosed the address so I wrote to the General Staff but they did not reply.

3. Someone from Hamburg added some other interesting pieces to complete the puzzle of the Finnish angel. He wrote: "In this century the Finns have already had to defend themselves against the Russian army three times.
The first time was during the War of Independence in 1917–1919. The second and third times were during the Second World War when the Soviets first attacked, then made peace and finally broke the peace treaty and attacked again. In all three wars General Mannerheim was the general of the Finnish army, directing his operations from Mikkeli, a town 230 km to the north east of Helsinki. The Swedish name for this town is St Michael, i.e., the angel Michael. Is this name a mere coincidence? Coincidence is something which comes to us from heaven and I see this name as an indication of the identity of the Finnish angel.

4. Finally, a Swiss woman sent me a copy of a chapter from a book called *Untergang und Verwandlung* (Downfall and Metamorphosis) by Edzard Schaper. It was published in 1952. To my surprise it contained a detailed description of the Finnish angel story. The

facts correspond with what was written in the first letter, but it also includes several other important details.

The place where the angel appeared was at Taipale, on the Karelin Isthmus. It was a sort of key position for the front. When this position had been taken it was possible to advance.

The first letter described how an angel appeared in blinding light. However, Schaper describes this slightly differently. He also mentions the blinding light, but then says that the light gradually became denser assuming the form of an angel.

This happens in several examples of personal stories about angels. He goes on to say that no further shots were fired until the break of day while the angels held guard. The exhausted soldiers all slept deeply.

Thus, the only thing that is lacking in this story about the Finnish angel is the account of an eyewitness. Even so, we should remember that even without an eyewitness account, the probability that this incident really happened is very great. There is such a thing as proof of the impossible: a Finnish victory was impossible and yet it happened. The Finnish victory was in itself a miracle. Therefore I opt here for the angel and against skepticism.

76 The next intervention from heaven took place on 13 May 1940, on Whit Monday at half past nine in the evening.

Nazi troops were advancing rapidly towards the Swiss border and the Swiss army was prepared for the invasion. Suddenly, soldiers and civilians in the Waldenburgertal saw a large hand in the evening sky, stretching over the region in a gesture of protection and blessing. Eyewitnesses related that it was not a peculiar cloud formation but a clearly identifiable, sharply defined hand of a man. The invasion which seemed irresistible, was unsuccessful. The Swiss did not attribute the protecting hand to that of an angel but thought it was the hand of Brother Klaus who had been revered as a saint in the area since the fifteenth century. A Nazi army rapidly advancing to a neutral country was not an unusual event in those exciting times. I remember the Secret Service, in which my father was involved, announcing in November 1939 that a Nazi army was rapidly advancing on our border. The invasion was expected at any moment. Father stayed awake for some of the night but nothing happened at that time. The actual invasion took place on 10 May 1940.

77 Curiously, the story about the big hand does not stand alone. On the day of Yom Kippur, 6 October 1973, Egypt and Syria simultaneously attacked Israel while the Israeli soldiers were praying for this great Jewish festival. This fourth Arab-Israeli war resulted in a terrible battle and initially it seemed as though Israel would be vanquished. The Egyptians broke through the Bar Lev line, which had been considered impenetrable, and took most of the eastern bank of the Suez canal. The Syrians stormed the Golan Heights, gained possession of Mount Hermon and quickly advanced 15 miles. The Israelis were completely taken by surprise and the traditional radio silence of Yom Kippur was interrupted to call every man to the front.

At that time there was an Israeli Health Officer who told the following story to a certain Mr Xandry, who in his turn published the story in *De Middernachtsroeop* (The Midnight Call), (June 1974). "The name and address of this officer are known to me". Here is his story: "Towards the end of the second day of the war we became aware of the hopeless position of our fighting troops. Everyone thought the end had come. The ammunition was nearly finished, an exceptionally large number of our comrades and friends in front of us had fallen, and almost all our tanks were damaged.

"The Golan front line which had been considered invincible, was taken by the enemy and the Syrians had started a bloodthirsty triumphal advance together with the troops allied to them. They seemed not to care that the number of soldiers killed in their ranks was even greater than in our own. They marched over their dead as though they were locusts. The ratio of Israeli troops to Syrian troops was approximately 1:10.

::As regards tanks the Syrians even had 20 to every Israeli one. Approximately 120,000 Arabs with 1,400 tanks were fighting against 12,000 Israelis with 70 tanks. In addition, the Arabs had the advantage of a strategically very well planned surprise attack which immediately caused the

Israelis to retreat 15 miles. Only the heart of our own country, the Jordan valley in Northern Galilee, was still behind us. Was it the end for our troops? Why weren't we receiving any military supplies? Where was the highly praised super-efficient Israeli army? Many people thought that the time had come when the Arabs would put paid to them. Poor Israel! Suddenly the Syrian attack came to a halt. What had happened? The soldiers that still remained were expecting the coup de grace but this did not come! In the middle of the advance the Syrians and their troops and tanks halted. Unbelievable! But we immediately responded to the new situation and with our remaining armoury we stormed forward, smashing the lines and penetrating their forces. The unbelievable happened: the enemy retreated just as rapidly as it had earlier captured our positions in expectation of victory.

"Then our small number of men put the gigantic enemy army to flight just as in the days of Gideon. Shortly afterwards our supplies and reinforcements also started to arrive and Israel was victorious again. This was my experience on the Syrian front. However, the question which intrigued us all is what happened in the Syrian ranks.

"Shortly afterwards I received information about this from one of our soldiers. He was still completely amazed by what he had seen. This is his story:

"'The Syrians were advancing. We saw the defence lines in front of us being mown down. Our lives were in jeopardy. Where were our supplies? We thought the end had come. Suddenly – I could hardly believe my eyes – a huge white hand came down from heaven between us and the Syrians. The hand placed itself calmly in front of the enemy battleline, stayed there a moment, and then very carefully pushed the Syrians back to Damascus. I was moved to the very depths of my soul by the majesty, beauty and absolute authority of this hand. What really astonished me is that none of my comrades saw what I saw, and yet everyone could see the effect of the apparition. The result was that we gathered our last strength and ammunition, and attacked. Our troops stormed after the Syrians with unbridled strength, although the army had been in utter despair only a short while before.

"'I did not hear this soldier's version of events until we

had been in front of the gates of Damascus for a long time. God had revealed himself in this way. Once again it was clear to me that the Lord of Lords had been the same since the exodus of Moses from Egypt and that He still protects Israel. He still fights for His people when the people call to Him in great need." I would like to emphasize the fact that the soldier who saw this is a Jew, a normal Israeli, who is neither particularly religious or an atheist. You could describe him as someone who enjoys the mercy of God without being aware of it. It appears that only this one soldier realized why the war turned to Israel's advantage." These were the words of the officer of health. It is reminiscent of the simple widow Klaas who was the only one who saw that Holland was protected.

Was this another version of an Old Testament story?

In the days of the Judge Deborah, Israel suffered under King Jabin of Canaan and his captain was Sisera (Judges 4).

In those days they really knew how to fight, for Sisera owned 900 iron chariots, the tanks of the time.

Nevertheless, Israel defeated Sisera, and the song which Deborah sang later contains the following line: "They fought from heaven, the stars in their courses fought against Sisera." (Judges 5:20). The following verse reads: "The river of Kishon swept them away." The rabbis explain this as follows. The heavenly bodies which determine the seasons and the weather on earth helped the Israelites against Sisera by causing the stream to burst its banks. Nowadays, meteorologists no longer believe that the stars can cause floods, but let us just assume for a moment that they are wrong, and that the stars are able to do this. This means that the miracle is even greater than a mere natural phenomenon. It means that the rabbis' explanation of the flood being caused by the stars had been determined at the beginning of time because the stars have a fixed path, and this happened just at the right time during the battle against Sisera.

All this is as irrational as the devout Jewish way of wishing someone good luck with the words "mazeltof": a lucky star. The positions of the stars are predetermined for all eternity so how can you express a wish that the stars will be in the right place for someone?

When you are concerned with heaven you always come up against this sort of paradox. This is the end of the section about angels in world history. There is no hard proof but then this does not exist in this field.

Before continuing with some personal wartime stories, I would like to discuss the aspects of angels which arose in the last few pages. We saw the angel as a fighter and for some believers this is difficult to accept. It is not compatible with the way they feel. They feel that anything that comes from heaven should be gentle and loving. I can imagine their feeling all too well, but from a Biblical point of view it is incorrect.

They might add that in the Old Testament there are many references to the Jewish God of Vengeance but the New Testament reveals the God of Love.

There are two things I would like to add in this respect:

a) Every devout Jew can tell you that the God of the Old Testament is full of love, sympathy and compassion. The Old Testament is overflowing with mercy and redemption. The "avenging God of the Fathers" was made up by people who have only read the Old Testament superficially. The God of the Old Testament is the same as the God of the New Testament. It is true that there is conflict but love is dominant.

b) The New Testament is certainly not sentimental. Jesus drives the moneylenders from the temple (Matthew 21:12,13). He says: "I came not to send peace, but a sword," (Matthew 10:34) and Revelations 12:7 even describes complete war in heaven where Michael and his angels fight against the dragon and his angels.

The New Testament, the 'book of love', is not without its conflicts. These two aspects – love and conflict – come up again and again. Conflict is part of our life, the whole of Creation is permeated with conflicts and we would do well not to avoid this confrontation when it is a matter of defending our integrity. Weakness is not a characteristic of a Christian. My archives contain a number of examples of fighting angels. They do not necessarily wield the sword at random, but their attitude is one of conflict. I would like to relate two stories here. They are not stories of war, but they do tell us something about conflict in Heaven.

78 A sculptor wrote to me that when he was four years old, he woke up one night. He sat upright in his bed and saw two enormous white cats on his left and right. They were larger than him and stared at him threateningly. He tried to call his mother but he was paralyzed with fear to such an extent that he could not make a sound. Then, through the wall, he saw a corridor lit up opposite him with someone coming down it towards him. He thought it was a beautiful lady. She was wearing a long draped white garment, lit up like moonlight. She walked slowly towards him, lifted him up and then laid him down again. The animals disappeared in a trice and he fell asleep contented and with his mind completely at rest.

He described the feeling radiated by this figure which he later learned to call beauty. The experience was not paralleled by any other experience of beauty in his life. The desire to have this experience again was his motivation for everything he did later on. At the same time he also experienced a sense of love which was quite unknown to him. This requires some explanation.

He grew up with two quarrelsome parents who often hit him and locked him up in a dark place several times. They never made so much as one attempt to talk to him. His parents were actually strangers to him. The "beautiful lady" showed him real love for the first time in his sad life.

I would like to remind you here of the striking similarity to some of the other stories which I have told.

Did this child have a nightmare or can this story be included amongst the true experiences of angels?

This certainly was not a nightmare. In that sort of dream the sense of oppression and fear just increases until you wake up.

Anyone who has had to wake a child from a nightmare knows how difficult it is. Even when they are half awake they can still remain trapped in the nightmare.

So what was this experience?

Bearing in mind the enormous and decisive effect that this experience had on the rest of his life, I do not think it is difficult to determine – this was certainly a true experience of an angel. Admittedly the gigantic white cats could be symbols of his threatening parents, but I am rather inclined to think that they were actually a type of demon, which had become visible.

The cat has two aspects. For the Egyptians it was a sacred animal because it was a reminder of a higher consciousness than our daily consciousness. This is the positive aspect of the cat. But anyone will remember the black witch's cat, and this is the demonic aspect of the cat. The cats in the dream were white, but perhaps they were unable to retain their black colour when they were in the vicinity of the angel. Whatever the case, we see an angel here chasing away demons, who therefore belongs to the army of the Archangel Michael.

The following story shows even more clearly the fight of good angels against demons.

79 The woman who had the following experience, had a spiritualist background. When she was converted, she was filled with terrible conflict. It was so bad that she was actually physically attacked, and thrown onto the ground.

(The reader should not shrug his shoulders in disbelief. I have seen one of my patients being given an enormous push by an invisible hand; this was a real case of possession.)

However, this woman relentlessly held on to the thought which was also the battle cry of Corrie ten Boom: Jesus is the Conqueror.

While she was still overwhelmed by this conflict her husband died, and shortly afterwards she woke up one night with an unpleasant feeling as though something was wrong. She turned on her bedside light and looked into the room. About a metre away from her stood a very large figure which seemed to consist entirely of white light. He looked like a young man and was unbelievably beautiful. She knew immediately that he was an angel. He stretched out his right arm in front of him. In his hand he held a sword and he pointed this in the direction of the corridor which led to the kitchen. She looked that way and saw the figure of a small woman: immediately she realized that this was a demon. It was wearing a white dress reaching down to the ground and a red cloak with a hood drawn over the head. She could not see the face, but the left hand covered the place where the mouth should be. The angel started to vanish into thin air and at the same time she felt something in herself saying: "Now you are awake and you have strength." The demonic creature slowly walked towards her, radiating an indescribably evil feeling. However, she did not feel any fear because she knew that she was armed with the Holy Ghost and she called:

"In the name of Jesus Christ, vanish and do no evil, go where you belong." At the moment that she pronounced the name of Jesus the creature disappeared.

I would like to point out that in this story it was not the angel but she herself who had to undertake the spiritual battle. This is very important. In the same way, good parents also teach their children to defend themselves in the struggle for existence. They do not mollycoddle them but allow them to do as much as possible for themselves.

I would also like to point out that the sword in the angel's hand manifests itself in other events as the power of the word with which the woman defeats the demon.

In spiritual regions, the sword does not serve for cutting off heads, but for using the word of God in the right way.

This brings us to the second part of this chapter:

INDIVIDUAL EXPERIENCES OF ANGELS IN WARTIME SITUATIONS

80 We will start one dark evening in the inner city of Haarlem. Complete darkness in a city is something which only older people will remember. During the war a moonless night meant total inky blackness. Everything was blacked out and not a ray of light would escape outside through the curtains. The street lights were off. There were no car headlights. No bicycle lights, nothing. On one of these cold, black nights, a woman was walking along a canal in Haarlem. She was on her way home and did not have a torch. In those days we often used a so-called "squeezy cat", a manually operated torch which ran on a dynamo and made a characteristic sound. This woman did not even have one of these torches and she did not need one, because she knew her way home like the back of her hand. First she had to pass the fish-

monger's stall and as soon as she had passed that she had to take eleven paces and then turn left and feel for the railing of the bridge which she had to cross.

When she came to the fishmonger's stall she carefully felt with her hand to see if she had passed it. Then she counted eleven paces, turn left and just at that moment she was grabbed and heard a voice saying: "Think of your children." Very carefully she felt for the railing of the bridge and realized with a shock that the bridge was not there. If she had not been grabbed she would certainly have fallen into the canal, and on such a dark evening there is no doubt that she would have drowned. Her mysterious helper did not say anything else and very carefully she started to look for the railing of the bridge. After a while she found it and crossed the bridge a little further on. She did not understand at all and the next morning, when it was light, she immediately went to look what had happened. Then she noticed that the fishmonger's stall had been moved. Her daughter told me this story.

81 The following story took place in the summer of 1942, outside Berlin, a city which was already being bombed at night. Three friends decided to spend a weekend outside the town. The first of these, who wrote me the letter, was called Dorothea, the second was called Miriam. These two girls shared a tent together. The third was called Gisela and she spent the weekend with her mother in a holiday home close to the place where the girls had their tent.

One Saturday evening, Dorothea, Gisela, Gisela's brother and her mother decided to go to a village festival a few miles away. They decided to walk. Miriam was tired and wanted to stay in the tent and go to sleep early. At the village festival, the four friends joined a group of villagers and some soldiers. They listened to music and danced and drank a few glasses of wine.

Later that evening the four friends walked back. Everyone was feeling merry and wide awake except for Dorothea. Although she had drunk just as much wine as the others it was as though she were drunk. Half-way back she even fell over and two of the others had to support her to take her back to the tent. When she got there she behaved in a strange way, for instead of getting into her own sleeping bag she wanted to join Miriam in her sleeping bag. Miriam was already asleep and reacted grumpily, but as she couldn't get any sense out of Dorothea she eventually agreed. That night the girls slept in Miriam's sleeping bag. I should just add that Dorothea is not a lesbian. She could not understand her impulse to crawl into her friend's sleeping bag, but it was so strong that she could not resist it. Despite their rather constricted position the two girls slept so soundly that they did not notice that Berlin was bombed again that night, and did not even hear that the anti-aircraft guns were firing at some distance from their tent. The next morning Dorothea woke up first and to her amazement she saw that she could see the sky straight through the canvas of the tent. Just above her own empty sleeping bag there was a large ragged hole in the tent. She crawled out of bed and saw a similar ragged hole in her own sleeping bag about waist high. The sleeping bag had a hole right through it. Meanwhile Miriam had woken up and the girls moved Dorothea's sleeping bag aside and examined the groundsheet of the tent. There was yet another large, ragged hole in this. Carefully they dug into the earth under the groundsheet and at some depth they found a large fragment of a grenade with sharp jagged edges.

In the war there were many examples of people who had been hit by fragments of grenades from the anti-aircraft fire. As I am writing this I can hear the strange singing noise they made as they came down. For a while you would hear that musical note, and then suddenly there was a hiss as it hit, followed by silence. If Dorothea had been hit in the stomach by this fragment, she would have bled to death immediately.

When she realized how she had escaped, Dorothea remembered her strange drunkenness which had not affected the other three members of the group. She also remembered her inexplicable urge to crawl into Miriam's sleeping bag. Admittedly she had not heard a voice or felt a guiding hand, but she realized that it had been a sort of heavenly drunkenness which had stopped her from rationally suppressing her impulse to crawl into her friend's sleeping bag with reason. Her drunkenness combined with her inexplicable impulse saved her from

danger. It was not for nothing that her name was Dorothea, "God's Gift."

82 The following story took place on 30 January
1945. A woman from Frankfurt on the Oder was
fleeing from the advancing Russian armies. During that
icy winter the Oder was frozen so hard that even the
heaviest cannon could easily cross it. There was nothing
between the people fleeing and the rapidly advancing
troops. The woman succeeded in catching the last train
leaving towards the west in the direction of Hannover,
Braunschweig and Seesen. After an endless journey with
many delays they were finally approaching Hannover.
In the middle of the night, when she had finally managed
to fall asleep, she was woken up by a voice which said to
her: "Get out of the train!" She noticed that the train was
standing still and looked out of the window. All she could
see was an endless snowy plain. Once again the voice
said: "You must get out!" She thought: "Surely I can't
get out here, in this snowy waste". But the voice repeated
even more urgently: "You must get out!" Then she
thought: "Perhaps they are my two dead sons, Christiaan
and Peter, who are warning me." So she picked up her
two heavy suitcases and her rucksack, opened the door,
threw the suitcases and the rucksack outside, jumped out
and sank into the snow up to her knees.
"You must be crazy," she said to herself, but she picked
up her luggage and walked over the tracks. After a while
she came to a street and walked down it. The street was
completely deserted and as she walked she saw that Hannover was being heavily bombed.
At last she saw a light burning in the distance and she
walked towards it. At half-past four in the morning she
finally arrived at a small station. This was a different line
and she found a train which by-passed Hannover to go
to Braunschweig. Thus, because of the warning she managed to avoid the fiercely burning city of Hannover
where she would have gone if she had remained in the
other train.
I received her letter in 1985, shortly after the publication
of the German edition of my book. In my mind's eye I
saw this lonely woman stumbling all alone through the
ice-cold snowy landscape. She had left everything

behind. Two of her sons were dead. The third had had to stay in Frankfurt because he had not been able to leave school and boys who fled were simply shot.

For the first time in 40 years I felt compassion for the Germans. This woman was one of the first who gave me the feeling that it was not an enemy who was walking through those icy, snowy wastes, but a human being, a victim of forces which were much greater than herself and to which she was subjected against her will. Here was a person who deserved compassion and who had suffered infinitely more than I had myself.

83 Another story took place on 13 February 1945. Again we see a woman who was fleeing from the Russian armies approaching from the east. Finally she arrived in Dresden. The city was packed with refugees partly because everyone was sure that Dresden would never be bombed. The city did not have concrete air raid shelters like Berlin.

As this woman stood in the street in Dresden, one of the hundreds of thousands of Germans there, she heard a voice behind her saying very loudly: "Just get out of here!" She looked around but there was no one there. Then she heard the warning again and it was repeated again and again. Though she could not see anyone she decided to leave Dresden. Her colleague said that she must be crazy but went with her to the station where overcrowded trains were leaving. With a great deal of difficulty she managed to get into one of the trains without even knowing where she was going. They were not far out of Dresden when someone called "Air raid alarm!" The train stood still and many people crawled underneath. Then so many bombers flew over them that it sounded as though the end of the world had come, and in the distance they saw the ancient beautiful city of Dresden burning fiercely. The city was completely destroyed in just a few hours. Later they heard that it had been bombed with phosphorus bombs and that many people had jumped into the Elbe like living torches. Her colleague asked her many times how she had known this was going to happen. She simply could not believe that it had been a message from above.

Later they heard from two others that exactly the same

thing had happened to them. One of these had even seen
her saviour. It was a man in uniform who had vanished
into nothing after uttering the warning.

The bombing of Dresden was one of the worst disasters
of the Second World War. The crowded city saw something which had never been seen before in air warfare –
there was a fire storm. As many people died as when the
atom bomb was dropped on Hiroshima. It was only years
after the war that we realized what happened there. Hell
ruled in many places in the world. In retrospect we
can realize that there were not just friends and enemies,
but seas of people suffering terribly, and amongst them
angels who would occasionally choose to save someone.
Why? Why is one person gently led away, like Lot from
Sodom and Gomorrah, while another jumps into the
Elba, a burning torch? 45 years after the fire storm the
fate of Dresden still makes me shiver. Occasionally there
are people who seem to attract angels. While some people
can go through life without even being aware of their
existence, other people come across angels several times
in their lives. The woman in this story has also had more
than one experience of angels. Another experience
follows below:

84 After the war Germany was in a terrible state. Half
of the country was destroyed and in some places
there was terrible hunger. This woman had been very
hungry for more than three years. She desperately tried
to get a job. One day she was walking in the pouring
rain looking for work, half starved, together with some
of her fellow Germans. Three Americans belonging to
the occupying forces asked them for their papers and a
fourth was sitting next to them eating some deliciously
smelling peas from a tin. He looked up and asked if she
was hungry. When she said she was, he immediately
handed her the tin and she ate the peas like a hungry wolf.
Then he asked her if she was still hungry. When she
nodded he gave her a packet of biscuits and she immediately ate half of them. He said she could keep the rest and
she looked for a place where she could hide them to
protect them from the pouring rain. When she had found
a dry place she looked up to thank him but he had vanished without trace. There was nowhere he could have

gone yet he was no longer there. She was completely confused about these events and did not understand how it was possible. It was not until much later that someone explained to her that she had met a guardian angel. We have not yet come across other angels in this book who give out food, but from the Bible we know that this is certainly possible. When the prophet Elijah was fleeing through the desert from the cruel queen Jezebel, after he had caused the downfall of all her priests, he fell to the ground completely exhausted and lost the will to live. Then an angel gave him cake to eat and water to drink (1 Kings 19:6,7). Just imagine being given cheese and biscuits from paradise.

Stories about angels are sometimes outlined very lightly. It is like looking at a Japanese print in which the artist has mainly made use of the void, the background of all matter. This is clear in the following story.

85 During the last days of the Second World War a twenty-year-old German girl was working in a children's home in the country. When the front approached the girls from the home had to try to take the children back to their parents as quickly as possible. This girl was entrusted with five children and she set out with them. She walked for six hours until she came to the village where she had to bring the children. It was evening and she had to walk back the same way. It was spring and the full moon shone in the sky.

She was in danger because the front could reach her at any moment. It was the night of 27 to 28 April 1945. The Russian and American troops had made contact at Torgau. Further to the north, the Russian army was already penetrating the centre of Berlin.

The woman reached a village and saw that it was full of soldiers, vehicles and cannons. It was not possible to get through and anyway this sort of situation was very dangerous for a young woman. As she stood there, hopelessly wondering what to do, a man in a soldier's uniform suddenly came towards her. He took her by the hand and led her through the chaos without saying a word. At the end of the village he let go of her hand and disappeared into the night without saying a word. By about midnight she had returned safely to the children's home. She always thought about these inexplicable things. She was one of those people who suddenly realized, when she had read my first book about angels, that that might have been what had happened to her.

The strange, silent behaviour of the soldier and the fact that she could not forget the incident for 40 years certainly pointed in this direction. Perhaps it was just an ordinary soldier, but one who was an angel for 10 minutes.

86 A similar mysterious event took place on 3 March 1945, involving a pregnant Dutch woman who was cycling down the Maliebaan in The Hague. Her dog was running along by her bicycle. Suddenly, she heard the wailing of the air-raid sirens. She cycled to the air raid shelter near the bridge as fast as she could, but meanwhile three bombs fell close by, probably aimed at the V2s in the woods in The Hague. She put her bicycle against the air-raid shelter but did not go in. More people were arriving every minute but they stayed outside to wait near the air-raid shelter until the all-clear signal was given.

Suddenly the group was addressed by a tall, slim man, wearing a long raincoat and a trilby hat which he had pulled down over his face so far that you could not make out his features.

He said that they should go into the air-raid shelter but they answered: "Oh, recently there have always been three bombs and then it's all over". However he said: "This time it's different. The planes are much heavier". All the twenty people who had now assembled, immediately went into the air-raid shelter, a large cellar with two main adjoining sections. As soon as the last one had entered, bombs started raining down. This was the bombing of the Bezuidenhout, which claimed many lives. Immediately after the all-clear signal, the woman crawled out of the air-raid shelter and could not believe her eyes. The Toernooiveld and the Prinsessegracht had been turned into a huge pile of rubble. There was nothing left of the Prinsesseschouwberg, close to the shelter. The Bethlehem hospital situated on the Prinsessegracht had also been hit. There was an enormous hole in the handlebars of her bicycle.

Everyone wanted to thank the man who had saved them. As he was not in their part of the shelter they decided to look in the other part but he was not in there either. Although this shelter was free-standing, so that they could see in every direction, there was absolutely no sign of the man. He should still be quite close but he was not there.

The trip back was terrible for her. She did not know whether her house had been hit. There was rubble everywhere and by the side of the canal in the grass there were several bodies of people who had been killed by the air pressure or by falling rubble.

Luckily she found her house unscathed but she still wonders whether for once in her life she had encountered an angel.

When I read a story like that it reminds me of an incident in the Old Testament.

Exodus 34 describes how Moses talked to the Lord on Mount Sinai and then went down to his people. His face was so radiant because he had been in God's presence that nobody dared to approach him. Moses had to tie a cloth over his face so that the people were not blinded by the glow, and every time that he met the Lord he had to do this. This makes me wonder what the people in the shelter would have seen if the man who warned them had taken off the hat which was pulled down over his face.

The next story reveals yet another form of heavenly intervention.

During the war thousands of people were taken to Germany as slaves. This was euphemistically known as "Arbeitseinsatz". Many people went into hiding as I did myself, but for others this was not possible.

87 In 1943 there was a young Dutch man who had exhausted all the possible ways of avoiding this Arbeitseinsatz. He felt very insecure because the bombing of Germany, and particularly of the German war machine, was constantly increasing, and you did not know whether you would come back alive. One day, just before he had to go, he felt a sort of vibration passing through his whole body, from the top of his head to the tips of his fingers and toes.

At the same time a quiet voice said to him quite clearly:

"No bombs will fall on your head." These words were uttered with such absolute certainty, that he felt every thought of death by bombing ebbing away. From then on he trusted this feeling completely.

In Germany he was in a small village outside Karlsruhe. One evening a circle of search lights appeared over Karlsruhe and this meant that the bombing would soon start. These circles of light were blown along by the strong winds so far that even the village where he was fell within the circle. Then fire bombs started raining down.
The fires were so severe that the whole surrounding area was lit up. Most of his friends were in the air-raid shelter, but he was on the first floor of their accommodation. Because it was so light he saw a fire bomb falling on a house on the opposite side of the street, point down. The bomb went straight through the roof, through the third and second floors, and then set the house alight from the first floor. In the reflection of the second floor windows opposite him he saw his own roof. Twice he saw a fire bomb whistling, point down, above his own roof but about one metre away from the roof the bomb turned horizontally and fell down next to the roof, once in the gutter where it did little damage and the other time over the gutter down into the street.

The same force that deflected an arrow which had already been shot from its course, also acted in the case of these fire bombs. Admittedly this man did not see an angel, but he heard one and saw what the angel did.

88 In the next story the young woman who was the main character did not hear anything, but she was saved in an extraordinary way. She had gone into hiding in the Peace Palace in The Hague with a group of people from the resistance. One day she went to see the man who made counterfeit stamps for their group. In her bag she had a cigarette holder with one cigarette, a handkerchief, money, keys, i.e., the ordinary things you find in a lady's bag. However, the cigarette contained a microfilm with information for the English and microfilm was also concealed in the handkerchief. She arrived at the house of the man who made the stamps, but she did not know

that the Sicherheits service, together with some collabor-
ators, had stormed the house. Thus when she rang the
bell she walked straight into a trap. A Dutch Nazi with
a gun immediately apprehended her and ordered her to
go upstairs. He walked behind her, poking her in the
back with the gun. Upstairs, her bag was taken away and
opened and she thought that this was the end and escape
was impossible. Microfilms for the English meant
interrogation, torture, a death sentence and execution.

The cigarette holder was put down on the table and
opened. It was empty. The keys, purse and everything
else was taken out of the bag but the security service was
not interested in the handkerchief.

She was transferred to the prison in Scheveningen, which
was known as the "Orange Hotel" during the war
because it was crowded with members of the resistance.
When she was locked into a small cell she thought it must
have been a case of dematerialization and realized she
would not die.

A few weeks later she was released for lack of evidence.
When she returned to the Peace Palace the first thing she
asked the housekeeper, who was also her sleeping part-
ner, was whether she remembered what had been in her
bag that morning.

The housekeeper slowly listed the various things. Suddenly she turned pale and asked: "Oh, that one cigarette,
didn't he see it?"

"No," she said, "it was gone, and I never saw it again."

This was the story as the woman told it to me at the
time. Later she wrote to me asking whether I had ever
heard of this dematerialization. Regretfully I had to
answer that I had never heard of it before. Since then I
have heard of entire cars and motorbikes which have
dematerialized. For forces which can achieve this, a cigarette must be a mere trifle. It makes you wonder in which
dimension the microfilm still exists.

One of the strangest things in stories about angels is that
it often happens that other people see a guardian angel
while the person who was protected is quite unaware of
this. The story of "The priest with two angels" springs
to mind. Here is another similar example.

89 A young man from the Netherlands was in Berlin in 1933. It was "Boycott Saturday", the day that the SS and the SD started to boycott the Jews in Germany for the first time. This young man was walking in the Friedrichsstrasse. He had deliberately bought a beautiful tie in a fashion shop run by two Jewish brothers.

That evening a friend of his said: "Who was that curly-haired fellow walking next to you this morning in the Friedrichsstrasse?"

He said that he couldn't remember any curly-haired fellow.

His friend explained that it was a fair boy a bit older than him. He replied that he still did not know who was meant.

He paid little attention to this incident and did not think about it although he retained a slight memory of it.

During the war he had to go out into the street one evening in 1944 with news from England. In those days we were not allowed radios and the penalty for having one was that your house would be set alight, but many people hid their radios and passed the news onto neighbours that could be trusted. The street was pitch black and he walked along the railings feeling for them. Unexpectedly, he walked into a few men who were standing in the street quite silently. They were Germans and they immediately started raging and swearing. This young man had acted in a German film, and in very cool and perfect German he swore at these Germans at great length. He shouted at least as hard as they did, and they were utterly astonished.

An acquaintance who lived quite near had heard the noise and looked out of his attic window to see what was happening. The next morning he saw him and said: "You must have been crazy to swear at those soldiers so loudly with that other curly-haired fellow with you and all that light."

This remark required some explanation. A man on his own would not have been so suspicious to those soldiers as two men walking in the street at night.

He started to explain to his friend who had looked out of the attic window that, in the first place, he had been on his own, and in the second place, there had been no light, and that's why he had walked into the soldiers.

His friend said that he was mistaken and that there was

a light as he had seen them both clearly and the other man had curly hair. At that moment the incident in Berlin came back to him and once he was home he said to his mother: "I have a curly-haired guardian angel." His mother listened to his story and was afraid. She said: "In God's name, be careful," apparently not realizing that he was cared for in God's name.

90 Not all angels are young and fair-haired. The following story took place in the 'Winter of hunger' of 1944.

A young woman who lived in Amsterdam was trying to reach her parents who lived in Haren in the province of Groningen. The boat to Lemmer was still sailing and she decided to take it. She was sitting in the saloon, together with a company of people loudly singing the popular song: "There at the Mill". She was not in a mood to join them because she was wondering how she would get from Lemmer to Groningen, now that there was no longer any public transport. So she sat by herself praying quietly asking God to help her.

The boat arrived in Lemmer very early the next morning. It was still dark. She stood on the cold, dark quayside wondering what to do next.

During a sailing holiday in the summer Lemmer is a very cheerful place. In wartime, in winter, just before sunrise, Lemmer is not a place where you feel very cheerful. She felt quite lost and lonely.

Suddenly she saw an old man standing next to her. He had a pale, sharp-featured face with serious eyes and he was dressed in a long black coat and a black broad-brimmed hat on his head. He did not introduce himself but merely stretched out his hand and pointed at someone who was walking a little further on, holding a lantern. "Follow that man," were the only words the old man spoke. Without hesitating for a moment she did what he said, and followed the man with the lantern.

They turned a corner and then another corner and she saw a lorry. She asked the chauffeur where he was going and the man said: "I am leaving now for Groningen." He gave her a lift straightaway and a few hours later she arrived at her parents' house. She was quite sure that God had sent an angel to her to show her the way.

It is strange that although she wrote me a letter about this strange incident in 1988, i.e., more than 42 years after it had taken place, she could still see the man quite clearly in her mind's eye.

Events which are related to heaven, have this quality. It is as though they are etched on the memory.

This is one of the rare cases in which the helper appears as an old man. Just as an angel often appears to a child in the form of a child, he can appear to a young woman as an old, trustworthy man, when she is standing all alone on an empty dark quayside at night. In the Bible the first words of angels are often: "Fear not!" These words do not always have to be spoken literally, they can also be revealed in the angel's appearance.

The local colour which angels can assume is often very pronounced. Jewish legends relate how Elijah always appears in the clothes of the time in which he makes his appearance. This is more than just a devout story.

Someone who sent me some very valuable material gave me a striking example of the way in which an angel had made adaptations.

This man is friendly with a Scots professor who told him the following story about his life:

91 The Scot was in China with a friend when the communist revolution broke out there. The two Westerners were taken prisoner and as people were hanged all over the place at that time – there were bodies dangling from every bridge – they feared for their lives.

However, they did not give up hope because they remembered the story from Acts 16, which tells how Paul and Silas were thrown into prison. These two had not given up hope either, but praised the Lord and sang psalms, until there was an earthquake in the middle of the night, which freed them from their shackles.

Therefore, the two Westerners sang and praised the Lord in their communist prison.

Suddenly the door of their cell opened and a mandarin in full regalia entered and asked them to follow him. He led them through many corridors to the main door of the prison and then walked along with them for some distance. On the corner of the street he bade them a friendly goodbye and then vanished without trace, as though he had dissolved into thin air.

My acquaintance asked his Scots friend whether he had ever published this story and was answered with typical Scots frankness: "Certainly not. Who would believe such a story in this country. The people have got over Christianity here!"

I am convinced that our Lord has a tremendous sense of humour and this story confirms my suspicions. In China a communist revolution was taking place. The proletariat was almost deified. Everybody tried to look as though they had come straight from the factory, still covered in dirt, or straight from the land, with dirty hands. Often this was the safest way, because during communist revolutions people were sometimes murdered just because they had clean hands. Then an angel of God appeared and what did he look like? Like a member of the sophisticated Chinese aristocracy. This is really one of Our Lord's jokes. Actually, I think that at a time when the aristocracy has complete power, for example, in the days of Louis XIV in France, angels probably appeared in the guise of peasants, servants or farm labourers.

The stupid thing about fanatical, political ideologies is that they completely suppress one side of life, and see their own side as the only one. On earth it is often a matter of choosing between the left or the right. Red or dead. This does not apply in heaven. Heaven consists at all times of one thing . . . and another, a right hand and a left hand, life and death. If too great an emphasis is placed on one side, you can be sure that heaven will provide a hint of the other side. The communist revolution in China was very un-Chinese. After all, it was the Chinese who produced the sublime symbol of yin and yang, the symbol which represents the unity of opposites. Inadvertently we have arrived in the communist world and I will continue with two miraculous escapes from the Russians.

92 The first story took place in Thüringen in 1945, just after the war. This part of Germany was occupied by the Americans, while the Russians were still occupying the adjacent area. Many people had fled to the West to escape the Russians.

A forty-year-old woman had left virtually everything behind on the Russian/American demarcation line, but when she heard the Russians had not yet arrived in her village, she decided to get her bicycle and fetch some clothes. The Americans allowed her to cross the border and she managed to get to her village where she spent one night. However, that night the Russians arrived and immediately the border was hermetically sealed. She started on her way with her bike but was stuck in the Russian zone, in a small village called Zell in der Rhön. All the people there were very frightened and excited. She heard that there was an escape route, but it led over a mountain pass. Thüringen is a country of mountains almost a thousand metres high. She asked whether anyone would be prepared to guide her through the mountains which were unknown to her, but neither her appeals nor offers of money had any effect. At one point she begged a woman to find someone who could help her. The woman looked at her with penetrating eyes and said three words: "Go, my angel!" This is all she said. With this sort of answer she did not know what to do, so she took her bicycle and started out on the mountain pass, trusting to luck. When she came to the top, a man walked towards her and said: "Madam, I will show you the way, but I do not want any money. Go through this clearing in the woods until you come to a farmhouse. When you are there you have crossed the border." This is what she did. It is a mysterious story. Who was the woman in the village who spoke the three words? What did she mean? Who was the man? How did he know that the woman with the bicycle was looking for a unguarded way across the border? The woman in this story wrote to me when she was 81 years old. She told me that she suspected that the woman in the village had been an angel. I do not know what to think. Perhaps there were two intuitive and helpful people, perhaps an angel working with man, perhaps two angels.

"There are more things in heaven and earth, Horatio, than are dreamt of in your philosophy," said Hamlet (*Hamlet*, Act I, scene 5).

I remember an old Indian medicine man in one of the books by Castaneda saying that he liked to sit in a place where there are many people. When he looked in a particular way – more or less like you look just next to things to see them well at night – he could see more figures walking round than the people actually there.

I happen to believe that Castaneda has made up all sorts of things, but it is certainly the case that the world "round the corner of our nose" is complementary to our own world. We do not observe it with our normal daytime consciousness based on the senses, but with the light, dreamy consciousness of the night. Perhaps that is why so many stories about angels take place in the dark or during moments of extreme fear or tension, when two worlds come together within us. Perhaps this is why the figures of angels so easily change form, just like the images in our dreams. An angel is certainly a reality, but the form in which we see him is often closely related to our own condition or to the person that we are.

In this book we have seen that in China an angel can even be a mandarin. As we saw, an angel often appears to a child in the form of a child or to a frightened young woman, alone on a dark night, as a fatherly old man, or to a woman in a city where bombs are falling, as a courteous soldier.

There is a strange intense relationship between the person who has the experience and the angel which appears. It would be interesting to investigate this. Although experiences of angels appear to occur rather arbitrarily, this is not the case. The experience was already in the person but suddenly becomes manifest. If on one side there are more shapes than people made of flesh and blood, on the other side, in these materialistic days, there are more bodies than people filled with spirit. Weinreb once expressed the regret that it has never been so crowded with so few people.

By saying this he was paraphrasing Diogenes (412 BC) who was once walking through Athens in the middle of the day with a burning lantern. When he was asked what he was doing, he said: "I am looking for a human being." Man is characterized by the fact that he has two sides. In Genesis I and II this is described by saying that man has two souls, the soul aimed at the earth, which is called the "creature" in our translations, and the soul aimed at heaven which is described as the "breath of life". Of all the living creatures man is the

only one with two souls. If he lives only on one side
he is not a full man.
If he is aimed only at the earth, he is not much better
than an animal or one of his own machines. If he is aimed
only at the other world, he becomes cut off from reality,
or fanatical.
Ideally the two sides are realized at the same time, the
aspects of day and night are united. This is why Diogenes
walked along with a lantern which belongs to the night,
although the sun was shining. The story told above is
full of symbolism. The woman in the village pointed at
the angel and the woman on the bicycle went up the
mountain. The man on the mountain pointed through
the woods to the farm to where a road led down to the
earth, and the woman walked down again. These are
respectively the divine soul (the woman in the village
who pointed up) and the animal soul (the man on the
mountain who pointed down). In addition, the whole
series of events led to freedom. It is only the co-operation
between the divine and the animal soul that allows man
to be free and to choose to do good in freedom, for
every form of one-sidedness leads to slavery. We will take
another look at the zone controlled by the Russians after
the war.

93 A boy whom we will call Kurt, had been taken
prisoner by the Russians and taken to the Ukraine.
This story took place in April, 1946. He was part of the
so-called International Work Battalions, which actually
consisted of Germans who had been taken prisoner by
the Russian armies advancing through Silesia and Brand-
enburg in February 1945, and had been put to work to
"carry out repairs behind the front". Thus they were
modern slaves just as we had been during the war in the
Arbeitseinsatz. Kurt's group initially consisted of 1,200
people who were crowded into a make-shift building
which had previously been an administrative building in
the Ukraine. The camp was called Schmerinka.
At the time that the incident described here took place,
this number of people was reduced by hunger, depri-
vation and hard work to 200. In the autumn of 1945 about
300 old weak people had been sent back to Germany and
the other 700 had died in the camp. The survivors

included some German women who had probably served in the German army. They were exhausted and at the end of their tether and like most of the men, they were in a state of total apathy.

Kurt was just 18 and was physically wrecked. Wasted to the very bone, he only weighed 35 kilos. His toes were frozen and he was covered from head to toe with scabies. He had lost his glasses and as he had very poor eyesight, he was virtually helpless. In other words, he was what was known in the German concentration camps as a "Muselmann", a living skeleton dressed in rags, whose eyes were full of despair.

In this state he was lying in the small clinic of the camp where only the terminally ill and the dying were sent, because there was absolutely no medical aid in the camp. These ill and dying people also had to fetch their food promptly from the camp kitchens, or they had nothing to eat at all. Kurt was much too weak to do this and for weeks on end he lay in a twilight zone between life and death. After the war many photographs were published of these poor souls, so it's easy to imagine what he looked like.

One day he had dragged himself to the back of the barracks for the sick, together with some of his fellow sufferers to feel the warm rays of the spring sunshine. Suddenly a fair-haired, red-cheeked healthy young girl, about 18 years old, appeared around the corner of the barracks, and passed from one person to the next until she stopped next to Kurt, stroked his arm and comforted him in a foreign language. Later he was told that she was Hungarian, but he could not really believe this, because people were always sent to the camp in groups, and there were no Hungarians there. In fact, nobody knew where she came from. Nor did anyone know in which hut she lived or where she slept. She certainly was not with the German women, because they didn't know her. Did she actually live in the camp? The only thing anyone knew about her was that she kept appearing unexpectedly around the corner. After this first encounter the girl regularly visited Kurt at his bedside. The strange thing was that she always walked straight towards him and never took any notice of anyone else. Yet from that moment, he and all the other people in the hut started to get better.

For example, one of the men had a nasty suppurating wound on his knee which had not improved because he was so malnourished. However, after a few days this wound closed up and the knee was healthy.

Because he was in a sort of twilight condition, Kurt cannot remember how long the girl's visits went on. It might have been four days, but equally it might have been four weeks. He thinks it was only a short time. To himself he called her his guardian angel. It was difficult for them to talk because she spoke to him in a hesitating Russian and he could only understand a few words. However, the important thing was that words were not really necessary. One day she brought him a wonderfully fragrant bar of the best quality soap. Actually it was absolutely no use to him because it was much too far for him to walk to the only tap in the yard. However, the psychological effect of this bar of soap should not be ignored. In the middle of the dirty, sombre environment it filled him with memories of cleanliness, relaxed baths, and a light and happy household. I think that this bar of soap helped him to go on a few more days, perhaps even more than a bit of bread would have done. Unfortunately, it was stolen the very next day. Soon afterwards the girl came to tell him that he was going to a hospital.

He found this quite incredible, for up to then no one had ever heard of German prisoners being sent to a Russian hospital. To his complete astonishment a commission arrived in the sick bay the day after this visit, to make arrangements for transporting the sick. When they came to his bed he heard someone say: "We cannot send him, he cannot be transported, we will have to leave him to die here." Straight afterwards the door opened and the fair-haired girl stormed in, followed by the camp commandant and the German translator. He only heard later on that the whole situation had reached a critical point as far as he was concerned. The handful of people, only five or six altogether, who were to go the hospital, were already standing by the door of the sick bay ready to go. His life was hanging by a thread. If his guardian angel was to save him, it was now or never.

Then he saw an unbelievable scene unfolding before his eyes. The girl threw off her thick Russian quilted jacket onto the floor and began to dance on it. As she was dancing she combed her fingers through her hair and scratched her face with her nails. At the same time she spoke loudly to the camp commandant and his translator, this time not falteringly, but in fluent Russian. He could not understand what she was saying at all, but she walked towards his bed and showed him lovingly that he should get up and get dressed.

Apparently the commandant had given his permission and he was saved. People rushed to help him, and as he had nothing to wear, a jacket, a pair of trousers and shoes were found in the mortuary. A few minutes later they opened the door for him and the men dragged themselves a few metres to the carriage of the train which was waiting for them next to the camp. The train journey took four days although the place where they were going was only 100 kilometres away. There they were taken to a perfectly run hospital for German and Hungarian prisoners of war. He was given medical aid and in September his condition had improved so much that he could be moved to West Germany. In December he was able to go back to school and prepare himself for his final examinations.

The crowning touch to this story occurred a few months after he left the camp. Just before leaving the hospital for West Germany people from his camp had arrived at the hospital. Of course he asked them immediately how the girl was. They said they did not know. As soon as he had gone, she had disappeared too. No one ever saw her again. They thought she must have gone to another camp. The unbelievable thing about this is that Kurt never spoke to anyone about this, not even to his parents. Now that he is 60 years old he realizes how improbable all these events were. He listed three totally improbable elements himself:

– a healthy, red-cheeked "Hungarian" who spoke good Russian, and appeared physically unscathed in a predominantly male camp;

– such a young prisoner who was taken seriously by the camp commandant in the middle of the Stalin period;

– good soap appearing as a gift in 1946 in the Ukraine when there was nothing there. This was impossible. Why such a useless present rather than bread? I have already

tried to answer that question and I would like to add a
few points here which seem significant;
– why did this woman always appear "around a
corner", the way in which angels usually make their
appearance?
– why did she behave so strangely when she wanted the
commandant's permission to let him go?
I think this reveals a good psychological insight. The
commandant was probably rather a primitive animal, and
was so fascinated by her performance that he was completely mesmerized and simply granted her request
unthinkingly. This worked rather like a conjurer performing his tricks on a stage, who constantly distracts
the audience's attention from everything he is doing. In
this case it was a matter of hypnotizing the man with her
bizarre behaviour so that the words that she was saying
went uncensored and he uncritically carried out her
suggestion of allowing the prisoner to go.
There are some strange things about this story. For
example, the imperfect Russian she spoke to him or the
incomprehensible language which was supposed to be
Hungarian. It is precisely these anomalies which make
the story so real. Heavenly encounters are often illogical
and contain mysterious elements which could only be
interpreted as a dream is interpreted. However, to do this
one would have to know a great deal more about the
people who had these experiences.
Kurt wrote to me that he felt more than ever convinced
– particularly because of the examples of angels he read
about in my first book – that she had been a real
angel.
When I reflect on this bizarre story once again, I come to
the conclusion that it really was a true angel, and furthermore, it was the angel which belonged to Kurt. The fact
that there were many people who saw her in these
extreme circumstances is not as strange as it seems. In
the concentration camps the doors to hell and the doors
to heaven were both open at the same time. How did the
camp commandant see her? This is a difficult question.
The commandants of these sorts of camps were usually
coarse and brutal men. Sometimes they were actually
possessed. It is a well-known fact that people who are
possessed often recognize heaven more easily than "ordi-

nary" people. In the New Testament there are some striking examples of evil spirits which recognized Jesus as
being the Son of God.

94 If anyone finds it difficult that this story was told
by a frightened semi-starving German boy, I will
contrast this with an experience told by a down-to-earth,
no nonsense man from Friesland. As some of you probably have not read the local newspaper in Leeuwarden
which contained this story and a large photo of this man
on 10 April 1984, I will summarize his story here. His
name was Tcake Spijkstra, the most Friesian name you
could imagine. If my Friesian grandfather had met him
in a café and heard his northern accent, he would immediately have asked him where he was from. During the war
and even just after it there was widespread diphtheria.
This is a horrible disease which causes a sort of membrane
to develop in the respiratory passages so that you can
easily suffocate. I have seen children being brought into
hospital with a rattle in the throat and blue in the face.
They have to have a tracheotomy straightaway, which
means a hole had to be made in the windpipe from the
outside. If this isn't done, they die. The disease can
develop very rapidly. When we were students we heard
about a surgeon who was eating in a restaurant with his
wife. The waiter who was serving them suddenly
grabbed his neck and started to turn blue. The surgeon
did not hesitate for a moment but placed the fish knife
that was in his hand on the waiter's throat, made a hole
in his windpipe, unscrewed the top of his fountain pen
to make a cylinder, put this in the hole and in this way
saved the waiter's life.

This story was probably told us so that we would never
forget the precise spot where the hole must be made in
the windpipe. It certainly helped because I could find the
exact place now.

This fellow Spijkstra was in a German prison during the
war, suspected of sabotage, and he was infected with
diphtheria there. His throat seemed to close up completely and he felt that he was close to death. Spijkstra
was not a man who went to church, but influenced by a
devout fellow prisoner he realized that it helped to pray
when you were really in need.

He was very weak and noticed that he could see less and less, when he was suddenly touched by a figure which he subsequently described as an angel. The figure stood in a beautiful light which radiated a great sense of tranquillity. The angel's hands were that of a woman but the eyes were those of a man. On one finger he wore a rectangular green ring. It was as though his eyes were saying: "What do you think of me?" Spijkstra immediately felt much better, and a few days later the impossible happened – he was cured.

It is important to point out an aspect we have not come across before in encounters with angels.

We have seen some people's inability to decide whether the angel was a man or a woman, but in this case the angel was described as having both male and female characteristics.

On earth we are all born bisexual, but one of these two sides is suppressed by the dominant side during the development of the embryo. This is why you are a man or a woman.

In heaven there is a unity of opposites. This is why Jesus answered the question of the Sadducees about the resurrection: "For in the resurrection they neither marry, nor are given in marriage, but are as the angels of heaven." (Matthew 22:30).

Another striking aspect of this story is the fact that the ring was green, i.e., the colour of healing. Furthermore, the ring was square.

On earth we are always concerned with cycles. Everything moves in cycles, the days, the seasons, the nights, the circulation of the blood. In heaven there are no cycles. Heavenly matters are often angular. The New Jerusalem is described as a perfect cube. From heaven we refer to 'the four corners of the earth'.

It is these details about the male/female characteristics of the angel and the description of the square green ring which identify Teake Spijkstra's angel as a true angel.

Thinking back to the Second World War we should not forget that there were theatres of war outside Europe as well. We will now take a look at Indonesia which was invaded by the Japanese, and where countless Dutch people suffered and died in the infamous Japanese camps.

95 A young Dutch woman was captured by the Japanese after the invasion of Java and imprisoned in Bandung. When she had been there for a number of days she was put into a cattle truck together with the other prisoners and after a journey of 36 hours she arrived in a concentration camp. In itself, a Japanese prison had been hell on earth. This was followed by the terrible transportation and then the horrors of the concentration camp. She was in a state of utter despair. During the night that she arrived in the camp she had to go to the toilet. She felt her way to the latrines in the pitch black.

Usually the camp latrines were no more than a plank over a deep cesspit.

Then something happened to her in the middle of the night which probably few people could relate because it is almost impossible to survive. She did not see the cesspit but slipped, lost her balance, and fell in. In her despair she decided to give up and drown. Her miserable life was no longer worth living. She seemed to have lost her will to live.

Suddenly she clearly heard a voice in her ear, a voice calling from above which asked her: "Do you believe in God?"

She realized straight away that this was the voice of an angel and she answered quietly to herself: "Yes."

Then the voice of the angel admonished her and warned her that she did not have the right not to do her best to get out of the terrible cesspit. "You cannot simply drown," said the voice. "You should not think that death will be a solution in this way, for those things you cannot face in this world, where it is your task to deal with them, will confront you again, and then in a situation which is much more difficult."

She was very shocked and called out: "Do you call this a life? This is terrible!"

There was no answer to her cry, there was only a lonely silence.

In this silence she came to realize the true meaning of the expression "the fear of God". It is not so much a matter of being afraid of God but a feeling of being pressed down by a tremendous weight of His holiness and greatness. This feeling was so overwhelming that she no

longer felt anything else, not even her sense of hope-
lessness.

She grabbed the edge of the cesspit to see whether she
could climb out, but it was full of slime and she could
not get a grip anymore.

Then she tried to find the bottom with her feet so she
could push herself up, but there was no bottom, only
slime and more slime and an overwhelming stench.

Again she was filled with despair, for she realized that
she would not be able to climb out by herself and in her
heart she called out: "Oh God, help me! I do want to get
out, but I cannot!" At the same time she was sinking
deeper and deeper into the stinking slime.

Suddenly she felt the finger of a hand under each elbow.
She was lifted from the cesspit as though she was no
heavier than a feather and laid down on the ground next
to the cesspit, where she fainted. When she came to, she
wondered where she was. She saw the dark sky with a few
stars above her and suddenly she remembered everything
quite clearly. How she had started out for the latrines in the
dark camp, how she had slipped and fallen in the cesspit,
and how she had been confronted with the voice of the
angel and with God's overwhelming holiness. However,
looking back, she remembered something else. At the
moment when she thought of the two fingers which had
held her under her elbows she saw not one, but two very
large angels in her mind. They were about two and a half
metres tall and she saw how they stood behind her and how
they each laid a finger under her elbows to lift her onto the
ground quite easily. She stood up weeping and went back
to the barracks. There she woke up her older sister who
was in the camp with her, and the latter immediately
dragged her to the bathroom where she was scrubbed clean
with water and kitchen salt.

Later this woman followed a long path towards her belief
which I cannot describe here. I would only like to add
that she became deeply involved with the underground
Russian church and that she intensely felt the difference
between the worldly luke-warm church of the west and
the suffering and conflict of the church which was
oppressed under the communist yoke at that time.
Anyone who would like to know more about this should

read the books by the reverend Wurmbrand. I thought
that this was one of the most beautiful and moving stories
about angels in all of my archives.
It reveals the sublime combination of spiritual rebirth and
physical salvation.
The story has such a wonderful structure that I would
like to analyze this in more detail.
The reverend Bullinger, the great Biblical scholar of the
last century, discovered that the Bible was written in
what he called: "Rhyming thoughts". These rhymes have
a structure which is either alternating or introverted, and
is often a combination of the two.
We are familiar with these patterns in ordinary poems.
In alternating verses the last verse of the lines rhyme in
accordance with the principle ABAB. and in inverted
verses they rhyme ABBA.
I will give an example of both these patterns.
Shakespeare's Sonnet 18 starts with the lines:
A: "Shall I compare thee to a summer's day?
   B: Thou art more lovely and more temperate.
A: Rough winds do shake the darling buds of May,
   B: And summer's lease hath all too short a date."
This is known as 'alternation', as the rhymes alternate.
(day . . . temperate . . . May . . . date)
Inverted rhyme is as follows:
A: When I have to rhyme
   B: My first attempts are rough
   B: For my muse is tough
A: And takes a lot of time.
Bullinger discovered how this principle of alternation and
introversion also applies in the Bible to the content of the
text. At first sight this is difficult to understand. I will
give two simple examples here:
A: It was a sombre winter day
   B: And the rain streamed down steadily
A: Josephine stared out through the window seeing
   nothing
   B: And tears poured down her face
It is possible to summarize these four lines as follows:
A: Sombre mood
   B: Rain
A: Sombre mood
   B: Tears

In other words, the content followed an alternating pattern.
Here is another example:
A: Pete got into his car angrily
   B: He raced off
   B: He screeched round the bend
A: And he felt his rage surging up white hot.
This can be analyzed as follows:
A: Rage
   B: Furious driving
   B: Furious driving
A: Rage
This time the content follows the inverted fashion.

We will now look at a more difficult text from Luke
11:34–36.
A: The light of the body is
   B: the eye
      c: therefore when thine eye is single
         d: thy whole body is also full of light
      c: but when thine eye is evil
         d: thy body is also full of darkness.
   B: Take heed therefore that the light which is in thee
      e: be not darkness.
         f: If thy whole body therefore be full of light,
      e: having no part dark,
         f: the whole shall be full of light,
A: as when the bright shining of a candle doth give thee
   light.
In thought rhymes rightly dividing the sentences is often
rather a puzzle but when that has been accomplished a
beautiful system of introversion and alternation appears:
A: The Light (or Lamp)
   B: The Eye (and the body)
      c: the eye
         d: the body
      c: the eye
         d: the body
   B: Light (and darkness)
      e: darkness
         f: light
      e: darkness
         f: light
A: The Light (or Lamp)

Thus opposite each other, we see the lamp at the beginning and the lamp at the end.

We see that the middle is determined by the eye and the body on one side, and by light and darkness on the other side. You could say that light and darkness are metaphors for the eye and the body. In this way we see that in terms of the content the whole text is determined by an example of inversion. But this is not all, for the two middle pieces B and B can be sub-divided into a form of alternation, of the eye and the body in (C–D) and in darkness and light (in E–F). This is a sort of signature of the Holy Ghost.

You have to look for it, but once you are aware of the pattern, it gives great joy. It is like a "graphological" proof that the text comes from the Lord, and was not thought of by people.

I had to provide this introduction to show you that the last story also contained this sort of poetic pattern.

A: The darkness
   B: Falling into the cesspit
      C: The angel asks a question
         D: The woman answers the question
      C: The angel admonishes
         D: The woman answers
      C: God speaks in holiness
         D: The woman calls for God
   B: She is lifted from the cesspit
A: The end of the darkness

The whole story is structured in accordance with lines which are also found in the Biblical text and thus it is reminiscent of the special feeling which God's word has for those who love Him.

I would like to add that there is no other book in the world which has this special structure.

Originally I did not wish to include the next story, which is not a story about angels. It is actually so alarming that I was rather afraid to include it. However, the reason why I did will soon become clear.

A few years ago a sweet young girl came to see me during my surgery. She was just 17 and had beautiful bright eyes and a funny smile. She had cancer and was completely bald as a result of chemotherapy. She had been told there was nothing else anyone could do, and she came to me with her mother to ask me if I could do anything because she did not want to die yet. She said this quite openly and innocently.

I gave her a prescription, and for a few months everything went very well. Her hair grew back and she gained colour and looked much better. She went on holiday abroad and enjoyed her life to the full. Suddenly she was afflicted with minor epileptic attacks.

Her family doctor gave me permission to visit her at home and she was still full of the will to live. One day just after her last attack she said to me: "I'm fighting," and she radiated self confidence. She repeated: "I don't want to die."

Three days later she died. It had been a case of euthanasia, "because she could not recover anyway". Her mother told me that she had resisted the first injection . . .

(*Euthanasia is legal in the Netherlands.*)

I cannot forget her. It is as though she is still looking at me. This experience persuaded me to include the next story.

The main character is a kind intelligent man who writes me very funny letters from time to time.

96 In October 1944, the south of the Netherlands had been partly liberated. The man in this story was still young then, happily married, the father of a son, a second child on the way and with a good job, although work had come to a temporary halt because of the lack of raw materials. This made him rather restless.

There was a notice in the newspaper asking people who could speak good French and English to supervise the transportation of food from French ports to the Netherlands. He was good at both languages and volunteered to go. However, time passed and two months after he had volunteered, Von Rundstedt attacked in the notorious Ardennes offensive. All the lorries were now being used to go to the front and there was no further transportation of food. However, because he had given his name, he was asked to act as an interpreter for the allied armies. He agreed and was allocated to a Scottish division.

In the night from 17–18 April 1945, this division advanced towards Bremen. It was said that there were still pockets of resistance there. In the early morning of 18 April they were quartered in a farm which was still reasonably well run. Scouts came to tell them that 88 mm grenades were

being shot from Bremen onto a road quite near to the farm.
There was a very clear pattern in these shots. Three grenades were fired on the hour. The Germans did this using a
compass because they were no longer able to see anything.
At seven o'clock there were three shots. They did no harm
because everyone had taken cover. However, at eight
o'clock and nine o'clock nothing happened. It was thought
that the Germans had given up. At ten o'clock no one took
cover but a grenade did explode.

The man saw that his chauffeur had been hit and was
lying in an open space. He was not moving at all. Was
he dead? Then a second grenade fell. It seemed as though
the chauffeur was moving after all. (Later this proved to
be because some of the fragments of the second grenade
had hit his body.)

The man thought very quickly whether he would try to
move the chauffeur away from the spot before the third
grenade fell.

He ran to the wounded man. When he arrived he saw
that he was almost dead, the two grenades had injured
him so badly that he could not live. His suffering was
terrible, but he had not quite lost consciousness.

Then the main character in this story did what many
soldiers had to do at the front. He took out his revolver
to shoot the chauffeur mercifully, he put his finger on
the trigger and at that moment he felt his hand being
stopped and heard a voice in his head which clearly said:
"You must not do that!"

He put the revolver back and then the third grenade fell.
He was seriously injured. He managed to bandage his leg
so that he was able to stop the bleeding. The danger was
past. The general appeared, saw his wounds and just said:
"Sorry, old boy". Meanwhile the chauffeur had died.
The man who wrote to me about this incident had to
have nearly 20 operations to mend his leg.

During these years this man learned to know God and
increasingly noticed that the Bible spoke to him. This
process started immediately after he had almost helped
the chauffeur to die.

There are two questions which arise in this respect:–
Why could he not shoot the chauffeur mercifully?
Who stopped him from doing this?

Why not shoot a man who is so seriously wounded that he has absolutely no chance of life and will die anyway a few seconds later?

Active euthanasia can be summarized as follows: "Now I will kill you."

Passive euthanasia is rather different. This involves no longer being involved in artificially prolonging life. This can be summarized in the sentence: "I will not treat you any longer."

The treatment for prolonging life can involve blood transfusions, chemotherapy, antibiotics etc.

Is there anything against active euthanasia?

This is a philosophical question. There are two possibilities:

A: A person belongs to himself.

If this is the case, he may resort to active euthanasia or ask someone else, for example a doctor, to do so for him. He is merely killing what belongs to him just as a farmer slaughters a pig.

B: A person belongs to God.

In this case he may only kill himself if he has been given permission by his Owner. A doctor could only consciously do this if he had been given permission by God.

Why was the man stopped from acting in the story told above, which was after all an extreme situation? I suspect that the reason is as follows. I do not believe that a patient or an injured person who is suffering without any hope of recovery, is worse off if he accidentally dies from an overdose of sleeping pills or painkillers.

Nor do I believe that it is morally reprehensible for a doctor to increase the dosage of a patient beyond the danger point in order to bring relief from pain.

I do not believe that in either of these cases the souls of the patient or the doctor are adversely affected.

However, there is a very fine distinction between increasing a remedy to such an extent that there is a chance that a patient will die, when this is necessary because the pain is so severe, and this in my eyes is suffering without sense so now I am going to kill the patient. I am convinced that man should not cross this boundary. But you should understand that this conviction comes from my own philosophy of life – I belong to category B. Let us take another look at this story to examine it very closely.

Suppose the interpreter in this story had managed to pull the trigger of his revolver. The chauffeur would have been relieved of his suffering. In this case his suffering would have been five seconds shorter.

I do not think that the interpreter was stopped because he should not have done this to the chauffeur. I am convinced that he was stopped for his own sake. The angel was saving him, not the chauffeur. It seems that consciously killing another person affects our soul and damages it. As we are not concerned primarily with our mortal bodies, but with our immortal souls, this damage to the soul should be prevented, and that is why the angel stopped him.

The second question was: Who stopped him from doing this? He himself says that it was an angel who stopped him. Others might say that the Lord had spoken. We are inclined to say it must be one thing or another. The Bible is much more subtle in this respect. For example, in Exodus 3:2 the angel of the Lord appeared to Moses like a flame of fire in the middle of a burning bush. But Exodus 3:4 says: "And when the Lord saw that he turned aside to see (the burning bush), God called unto him out of the midst of the bush, and said, Moses, Moses." We see that the angel and God use each other. The Jews say that when God acts we see an angel. Thus the question who it was that spoke to the interpreter is actually a question about the meaning of words, and this applies to a greater or lesser extent to all stories about angels. God acts and speaks, and we see or hear angels.

We will now leave the Second World War and describe an experience of an angel which has occurred in many places rather like the "priest with two angels". I have called this phenomenon the *white guard* and here is a story which is typical of this sort of experience.

97 During the war in Vietnam hundreds of people were walking silently by a river one night. From time to time the leader would whisper his instructions which were obeyed silently.

They came to a number of rafts in the river. The people, altogether 1,400, crawled onto the rafts with their scanty possessions, cast off and without making a sound, drifted down river. Who were these people and who was their leader? The leader was a Vietnamese man named Saul and he was an evangelist. His fervent sermons had led the inhabitants of five villages to become converted to Christianity and from that moment their lives were in danger because the Vietcong were ardent communists who exterminated all Christians. When they caught a Christian he was often buried alive.

The Vietcong had learned that no fewer than five villages had converted to Christianity. They had surrounded these villages and were ready to attack them, but Saul thought ahead and therefore these rafts were lying ready in the river, like a modern Noah's Ark. That night all the inhabitants of the five villages had crept through the Vietcong lines which were not completely watertight, and now they were floating downstream.

Near Danang, close to an American garrison, they built a new village together. It was not long before the Vietcong found out where they were and after a while the new village was also surrounded by a strong concentration of heavily armed guerrillas who were hiding in the jungle. This time there was no escape and the Americans could not protect them either because they had their hands full. Thus, the village was hermetically sealed and no one could go in or out. The inhabitants started an uninterrupted vigil of prayer in the recently built church. They prayed for three days and three nights. The Vietcong retreated quite unexpectedly.

A little later one of the Vietcong guerrillas was wounded. He ended up in an American hospital, where the story of the village which had been liberated in such a strange way, was well known. The doctor who was treating the man gained his confidence and heard that he belonged to those who had held the village in an iron grip.

"Why didn't you attack the village? It was not armed. They were quite impotent!" asked the doctor "Don't you know?" said the Vietcong soldier. "We couldn't do anything while large groups of soldiers in white uniforms were regularly patrolling the village."

In fact, there were never any soldiers in white uniforms during the Vietnam war (from *Een Nieuw Geluid*, 1968).

98 Here is a similar story though with a slightly different content, which took place in Rhodesia. It is set in the 1970s and was told to me by E.C. Wesson.

A farmer's wife was hanging out the washing. Terrorists had been ordered to shoot her dead, as was happening everywhere. The woman didn't know anything about this but later some of the terrorists were taken prisoner and one of them related how they had been ready to attack the farm just as the farmer's wife was hanging out the washing. The reason they had not done so was because of the enormous soldiers dressed in white who were constantly walking between her and them.

99 There is another story told by Wesson about a group of guerrillas who wanted to attack a farm in Rhodesia. There was a farmer in the farm who was praying at that time. When he wanted to stop, a voice told him to go on praying. He did not know why, but he obeyed. The guerrillas who were caught, said later that it was exactly at that time that they had been ready to attack but were unable to because the farm was completely surrounded by soldiers dressed in white.
The stories recounted here were told to Father Wesson by eyewitnesses. Therefore they are not first-hand stories like most of the stories about angels in this book.

100 In the book by the reverend Lindeboom which I mentioned above, *In Het Uur der Bezinning* (In the Hour of Reflection), there is an almost identical story about a missionary called Van Asselt, who went to the extremely dangerous Batak area in Sumatra. The Bataks repeatedly tried to murder him but again a double line of guards with shining faces surrounded his house and prevented the attack. One of the Batak warriors told him this story himself. There is another almost identical story from China.
In all these stories it is striking that the people who were protected were quite unaware of what was happening and only the attackers saw the guardians. What is this phenomenon? Is it "an angel by the motorway" which was recently referred to in a magazine as "a ghost by the motorway"? I do not think so. The protection of Christians by angels runs through the history of Christianity like a red thread. However, again some people are saved while others are actually murdered. This has always been the case and we do not know the reason. What do we know? Why does a

good soul who is always ready to help anyone, die at an early age, while another nasty piece of work continues to taunt his family until he is 90 years old?

The apparent arbitrariness which seems to apply with regard to angels saving people should not be a reason to shrug your shoulders and reject the story. If this were the case, we would have to reject all of life. I certainly would not trust stories about angels if they only happened to good people. If this were the case, it would be logical to conclude that they were not true.

The chapter about angels in wartime situations concludes with this series of white guards. Even in this series of highly similar stories there is a great diversity. The main theme is the same but the details differ.

This means that we are concerned with real life. Everything in creation reveals a uniformity in its general theme and an infinite variety in the individual execution of this theme. A leaf is a leaf, but no two leaves on one tree are exactly the same. A wolf is a wolf, but their characters are all different. A face is a face, with eyes, ears, nose, mouth and cheeks and yet, we can recognize one beloved face from all the other people on earth. In the same way we can see this typical characteristic of creation in the stories about angels – they have a general structure and yet each encounter with an angel is a unique event. In the last chapter I will try to summarize all this material. It is an enormous subject. One of the things which has struck me is the relation between experiences of angels and the experience of being close to death. It is difficult to put your finger on it precisely, but there is a certain connection. Perhaps it is like this, that in the angel experience the angel comes looking around the corner, while by the near death experience the human being looks around the corner. In both cases the door between this world and the other world is wide open. It is good to get to know that door. I will return to this later.

---

* "During the battle a war correspondent of the *London Evening News* sent to his paper a story about bowmen from the time of Henry Vth who came to help the British soliders. The public thought it was true. There are some similarities with the stories in this book but also great differences."

CHAPTER 6

EVALUATION

This book describes 101 experiences of angels; 68 of these were experienced by people who wrote to me personally or whom I have met; nine of them were told to me by close members of the family or intimate friends of those who had the experience; the rest consisted of well-documented stories published in books, magazines and newspapers.

I received most of the letters in the years 1984–1987. In connection with writing this book I wrote a letter to all the people who had told me about an experience with angels, asking them whether I could use their story, and also asking them if they could tell me to what extent their life had been changed by the experience.

Although it was five to seven years since most of these people had written to me about their experience, I soon received replies from a surprisingly large number of people.

More than two-thirds wrote back to me straightaway. Not only did they give their permission for me to use their story but they also wrote at length in reply to the question whether their life had been changed. They answered this question seriously, giving many details.

There were also moving letters from people who had been concerned that their story would disappear with them, and were glad that it would be recorded for future generations. For them my letter about the new book was like an answer to a silent prayer. Nine of the people have died. I am grateful that I was able to use their stories. Two people did not give an address in their first letter. Four people did not reply to me in 1991.

It was difficult to decide what to do with their stories. In the end I decided to retell them in my own words, giving them a strict guarantee of anonymity. I hope that if they read this book they will write to me. Almost all the people – with very few exceptions – told me that their lives had been fundamentally changed by the experience. I studied their replies thoroughly and compared them to their original letters. In doing so I came to the following tentative conclusions:

THE PERSON BEFORE HIS EXPERIENCE WITH AN ANGEL

Experiences with angels do not occur to people by chance. There is a sort of run-up to the experience. The best way to describe this is by using a sentence from one of the letters: "When I was a child I did not feel at home on this planet". This feeling of "being strangers and pilgrims on earth" (Hebrews 11:13), is one of the characteristics of the people who wrote to me, which can be found in the letters. They were often lonely and sensitive when they were children. As adults they are quite often people who do not entirely fit in. Often they are simple modest people who quietly go their way in their own circles, at the same time fitting in and not fitting in. There is something about them which sets them apart, they are not one of 12 in a dozen, they are the thirteenth. The door which swung open for them when they encountered an angel, was already ajar.

THE EXPERIENCE ITSELF

We have seen a number of examples of several witnesses who saw the same angel, but it happens far more often that there are two people, one of whom sees the angel while the other does not. Once again I think this shows that you do not encounter an angel in the same way as meeting your neighbour. People who see the angel have 'opened' an eye for a moment to see what is not visible to most people. They can swear that they were completely conscious, and yet it was slightly different because they seemed to have an extra sense – a third eye so to speak – which opened to see what was invisible. That is why when people encounter an angel they behave differently from what you might expect. Just imagine what I would do if I walked into my garden and found an elephant. I would call my wife, phone the police, warn the neighbours, in short I would be very active. People who meet an angel, which after all is just as unusual as coming across an elephant, do not do any of these things. The experience is quiet and intense, and in most cases no words pass between them and the visitor from heaven. An encounter with an angel is essentially different from an encounter with something or someone from the outside world, even if that is an elephant in your garden. I should add that I have used that particular example, because I had rather a strange lady in my practice who declared that she always saw an elephant in my garden.

THE SHORT-TERM AFTER-EFFECTS

I have already mentioned these in my first book about angels. We often find that people have a constant sense of bliss for several weeks. In a few rare cases there are also feelings of confusion and anxiety. It is as though the soul has undergone an earthquake and the tremors can be felt for a long time afterwards. These are characteristic reactions to the experience.

THE LONG-TERM AFTER-EFFECTS

The majority of people wrote to me that their lives had been fundamentally changed. One of them wrote: "The incident has increasingly become the central theme of my life." What actually happened to these people? Every person is unique, and similarly every experience is unique, but nevertheless I think there are seven main categories which can be distinguished in these stories. The changes in the lives of these people took place in the following areas, and we should realise that in most people it was not just one, but several of these areas which were affected.

FAITH

Many people wrote to me that their faith had been strengthened or confirmed. One man wrote: "From assuming that God exists, to knowing that God exists." This is almost the same sentence used by Job when he met the Lord: "I have heard of thee by the hearing of the ear: but now my eye seeth thee." (Job 42:5). The people experienced that their contact with God had become personal. Biblical texts came alive. Miracles described in the Bible became real because these people had experienced a miracle themselves. In this context it is striking that people with a Protestant background often described a deeper relationship to the Bible, while people with a Catholic background sometimes referred to a more intimate relationship with Mary. This seems rather strange to an elderly Protestant.

This aspect reminded me of something which Elisabeth Kübler-Ross said. Dying children never see Mary if they are Jewish, or Elijah if they are Catholic. This is another example of the singular flexibility of heaven, which modestly adapts itself to our own faith. Clearly heaven does not have a tendency to compartmentalize.

In one of the replies I received, I came across a terrible story. The woman who wrote to me was being treated by a psychotherapist whom she trusted completely. They were working on certain problems and one day this woman very cautiously related the story of her wonderful experience with an angel. Her therapist identified this as a sign of a schizoid personality. In other words she was told that she was a split person.

This therapist's view is not just slightly incorrect, it is terribly wrong. If there is one thing that is absolutely clear, it is that an experience of an angel results in greater inner unity. It is exactly the opposite of a schizoid development which increases the split in the personality. The person who reacted wrongly in this case was the therapist for she had such a rigid framework of ideas that she had to force her client's angel experience to fit in with that framework.

Another thing which struck me was that none of my correspondents refers to a closer relationship with the Church. Those who were members of a church did not stop going after their experience, but it was as though they realised the relative nature of any human organization. They had been confronted with the world which forms the basis of our faith, and were therefore less rigid in relation to those who merely talked about this. Is this the reason that the Church has always been rather suspicious of mystics? The Church makes some very absolute statements about itself, and mystics tend to take such pronouncements with a pinch of salt.

Whatever the case, an experience of an angel places a person with both feet on the rock of faith. The certainty resulting from this is not merely a quiet acceptance. For the woman mentioned above, it actually led to a great restlessness and an energetic search for God. This is not an unusual development. Jewish doctrine describes a priest as someone who is always restless. He wanders restlessly through life because he knows that he is a stranger. However, this restlessness is quite different from the rat-race of modern existence. It is a more "tranquil restlessness".

FINDING THE MEANING OF LIFE

After the experience, life had a meaning, and for many people this was quite different to the state in which they had been before. This is an extremely important development. One of the greatest evils of the modern age is the sense of purposelessness that many people feel. They feel like a cipher, mass produced, disposable. After an experience of an angel they can no longer feel like this. There is a sense of certainty regarding their unique quality, their individual existence and the purpose of everything that happens to them. As one of my correspondents said: "This leads to a sense of peace and invulnerability." This does not mean that nothing unpleasant can happen any more, but whatever happens, you are invulnerable inwardly. It is the quality which dictators hate most. When they meet someone with this quality, they start torturing them. Religious persecution always involves this. There are few experiences with such healing powers as the rediscovery of the meaning of life. It is not for nothing that people who have encountered an angel are able to help those around them.

UNITY, LOVE, MYSTERY AND INTEGRATION

These are all names for something which does not have a name but, which is concerned with God Himself.
Many people told me that they had a new sense of life.
One person said: "My soul is healed."
Another person said: "I am more separate from the world."
A ninety-year-old woman said: "I have become deeper."
Many people said: "I feel enlightened."
A dear old lady sent me a photograph and said: "I am young."
All of them noticed that their capacity for real love had increased.
The feeling was so difficult to describe that it led to some strange utterances. One woman said:
"I am myself and my other self." (The earthly and the heavenly twin).
Another person said: "I know that everything that is created is part of a whole." She was not the only one who described this. The experience of oneness is essential in this wonderful new sense of life. It is difficult to express this in words and many people do not quite succeed. One sculptor said: "I can only really express it in stone." Stone has always traditionally been an image of eternity.
Searching for the right words it is occasionally described as a "cosmic" feeling. "The mystery has come closer."
"The invisible has been confirmed for me."
This last example is reminiscent of the definition of faith: "Faith is the substance of things hoped for, the evidence of things not seen." (Hebrews 11:1).
The woman who saw an angel by her mother's death bed described the sensation very beautifully:
"I have a feeling of great inner certainty that there is a thin wall between this world and the other world." This feeling of an all-embracing world is also expressed in the ability to assimilate negative experiences in life better. People realized that disease, suffering and disasters fit into the pattern in a strange way, just as the shadows in

Rembrandt's paintings revealed light more clearly.

Again and again the immense pattern of an all-encompassing oneness is emphasized. One woman expressed it in the following terms: "I feel a link with all the early Christians. Experiences of angels are not meant personally but are a sign of God's realm for everyone. I have found that there is an increased power of observation in every field. The experience of angels fits in this as though it is part of a huge mosaic."

This is the tapestry described by Corrie ten Boom, in different words.

Swedenborg said something similar. He compared life to the pieces of coloured glass which are randomly arranged in a kaleidoscope. When you look from the outside you do not see anything special. But when you look into the kaleidoscope you see the most beautiful mosaic with the help of the specially angled mirrors.

The sense of unity which is typically felt after the experience of an angel is one of the most fascinating and permanent effects. I am grateful to the many people who wrote to me about this, for the pains they took to try and express something for which there are no words.

SPECIAL GIFTS

It is extremely interesting that some people appeared to have special gifts after their experience, which they retained for the rest of their lives.

The Bible mentions nine gifts which the Holy Ghost granted mankind: wisdom, knowledge, faith, healing, the working of miracles, prophecy, discerning of spirits, diverse kinds of tongues and the interpretation of tongues (1 Corinthians 12:8–11).

Several of these gifts are granted after an encounter with an angel.

Some of the people had received the gift of prophecy; they knew what was going to happen. Prophecy is more than merely seeing into the future. As the ninety-five-year-old woman who got out of the train into the snow, describes: "I can take a look behind the material world." Other people received the gift of healing. By laying on hands or praying they could cure all sorts of illnesses. Yet other people noticed that their perceptions were changed.

They had acquired an improved ability to tell whether someone was being spiritually truthful or not.

There is so much pretense, kitsch and deceit in the field of religious faith, that you have to wonder whether what you can see or hear is really true in everything you come across.

In ordinary life we do this all the time: Is this apple ripe? Is this pure wool? Who paid for this scientific article? Does that politician really mean what he is saying? With regard to faith it is more difficult to discern the truth, because we are dealing with an invisible world, and that is why we need this special gift to distinguish the truth. Also with angel experiences we need the gift of the discerning of spirits.

This is absolutely essential.

Let us suppose that I am sitting in my room on my own one evening. I am rather sleepy and a lamp sheds a soft light. Suddenly the room is filled with a bright light and an enormous angel appears before my astonished eyes. He reaches up to the ceiling with eyes like fiery coals, his fair hair waving down on his shoulders. He is dressed in a long white garment tied with a purple belt and he is wearing golden sandals on his feet. In a thundering voice, he says: "I am the Angel Gabriel. You have been chosen to give a message to the world. Tell all mankind that the time of mercy is past. The era of vengeance has come. Vengeance for the persecuted faithful. Vengeance for the destroyed environment. Vengeance for your restless pleasure seeking. For two thousand years Christianity has spread mercy but the time of judgement has come, because you refused to listen. There will be a time of war. Teach the people to have no mercy for the enemies of the faith. For 40 years you shall hate and persecute your enemies. Retribution will come to anyone who has followed the false teachings of the anti-Christ. You may be one of those who will sweep the world clean with a broom of fire. Kneel down before me and swear that you will carry out your task faithfully!"

I would hope that at such a moment I would keep my marbles and reply: "Go and tell that to the marines you evil spirit" because it is written "Love your enemies, do good to them which hate you, Bless them that curse you, and pray for them which despitefully use you." (Luke 6:27).

Then the angel before my eyes would change into a rather unpleasant smelly little man with a grey face and a ragged goatee beard, dressed in a dirty black suit. He would give me a venomous look and disappear leaving the stink of the sewer behind him.

It is actually the case that invisible beings which are not well-disposed to mankind can also appear in the form of shining angels. We should always test every experience. If an angel does not say anything, we can do this by looking critically at the influence of the experience on our lives. Was it a positive or negative influence? Did my tolerance and understanding increase or diminish?

If the angel does speak, it is best to compare his words with the Bible. Even Jesus used this method during His temptation in the desert (Matthew 4:1–11).

This warning to test the experience should not be taken lightly. Sometimes the devil can be a charming crook who flatters your vanity and at the same time interferes with your integrity. He is false by definition. Even if your faith was strong, he can take it away without your noticing and replace it with false spiritual values.

Amongst those who received gifts there were some who had instructive visions. Some saw the country where they lived as a large living panorama below them. The effect of this experience was that they became aware that they were integrated in a much larger whole. True experiences of angels always lead to a greater unity.

In this context I am reminded of Vanya, the Russian soldier who saw the New Jerusalem, just before he was murdered by the KGB because he was a Christian.

I think that these visions should be included amongst the gift of wisdom. It is knowledge which comes to us as a manifestation, and not through our intellect.

In summary, the approach of one of God's angels appears to be sufficient to bring the particular gift which that person needs most, both for himself and for the salvation of those around him. Gifts are not scattered liberally – they fit each person as a key fits into a lock.

THE DISAPPEARANCE OF FEAR

Many people wrote to me that from the time of the experience of the angel they no longer felt fear. In particular their fear of death had gone for good, but so had the fear of illness, operations, and even things such as frightening traffic situations, were seen in a more relative light. When you see the enormous role which fear plays in life, it is clear that this is also a great change in spiritual life.

Why is it that an encounter with an angel, which often only lasts a few seconds, can drive away fear?

"Perfect love casteth out fear", according to the apostle John (1 John 4:18).

It is clear that an angel who is entirely filled with God's love, can banish fear for a whole lifetime.

In his book *The Great Divorce*, C.S. Lewis said that the whole of hell is actually so tiny that a butterfly in Heaven could devour it without getting indigestion. Everything from hell has a shrinking effect. Fear also has a constrictive effect. People who had experiences of angels discovered a great sense of faith.

A man wrote to me that since his experience he had felt a constant sense of joy and was in a permanently optimistic mood which did not even abandon him in a crisis. This was the man who was saved by the fair-haired Hungarian angel in the Russian death camp. It was only after their experience that many people learned the true meaning of praise and gratitude and prayer. Their fear of life was replaced by a great love of God and their fellow men. There was no room left for anything else. You often recognize these people by their eyes. They have tapped a source of joy which seems to bubble up like living water.

A SENSE OF DIRECTION IN LIFE

Many people indicated that after their encounter with an angel they felt that their life had a sense of direction. When they arrive at a crossroads, this direction shows them the way they should follow. They are not ashamed to ask the Holy Ghost for help and know they are protected on their way. It is actually a pity that so few of the people who lead us use this help, which is always present. Just imagine that the government of the country, local government and town councils, the leaders of big industry asked the Holy Ghost to lead them. Our world would become quite unrecognizable at a stroke.

Since Thomas More wrote his *Utopia* there have been several such devout wishes. Unfortunately, for the time being we will have to put up with the division between those who have good and inspired ideas but no power, and those who have power but no good inspired ideas, and who do everything they can to suppress any new ideas that they encounter.

In principle most of the great problems in the world have already been solved, but the solutions have not yet been carried out because the people who govern over us are not big enough.

CHANGE IN DAILY LIFE

Any change in feelings, strengthening of belief, special gifts, visions and love would be pointless if they did not have any effect on life in practice. That is why it is extremely gratifying that the people who wrote to me almost without exception said that their lives had been changed in a practical sense. They found they had the courage to pursue their ideals regardless of the social consequences. The man who felt a constant sense of joy is someone who does everything he can to improve the environment and has obviously come across the usual problems in his endeavours. Many people found a sense of fulfilment in helping others. One woman literally said that she was able to love people better now that she knew what it was like to be loved herself. The proof of the pudding is in the eating. True experiences of heaven are always translated in practical help to the immediate surrounding world. Saints are never vague wanderers. I am privileged that I have met several real saints and they were always down-to-earth, active and practical people. To summarize, it must therefore be said that experiences with angels have a very positive influence on the people who had the experience.

You could say that this change in life is characteristic of the truth of the experience.

Can this positive change be summed up in few lines? What is the fundamental transformation which takes place in the human personality? The person concerned has acquired an open structure instead of closed structure. In psychological terms, he no longer lives in a house with a closed roof, but in a leafy hut in which you can see the sky through the roof.

It is strange that Christians are not familiar with the Feast of Tabernacles. Apparently there is a prediction that this festival will be celebrated by Christians and Jews together at the end of time. Perhaps the growing number of people who have had experiences of angels serve as good omens for this future communal joint festival.

When I wrote this chapter and listed the conclusions I have come to, the long-term effects of experiences with angels seemed vaguely familiar. I wondered whether I had ever come across anything like this before and suddenly I remembered the book by the French journalist and author Van Eersel, who was one of the first people to examine the permanent effect of the experiences of being almost dead.

In Van Eersel's book, *La Source Noire* (The Black Source), he describes these after effects and they reveal the striking similarity to what I have described as the long-term effects of experiences with angels. Van Eersel also came across the slight distancing from the world, the complete lack of fear of death, a strong faith which is in no way fanatical or dogmatic, a slight tendency not to adapt to the rest of the world and strange spiritual gifts. He suspects that a change of consciousness is taking place on our planet. If this is true, let us hope that it happens quickly.

Just before this book was printed I received a copy of Charles Flynn's book about the experiences of people who have almost died. This book strikingly confirms the correspondence between the after effects of these near-death experiences and experiences of angels.

This changing consciousness is taking place quietly and unobtrusively. And yet – if the signs are not misleading – they will become more influential in the years ahead.

In the first place, there is a growing number of people who have had near-death experiences as a result of modern resuscitation techniques. In the second place, I get the impression that there is a great increase in the number of spontaneous experiences of angels.

All the people who experience these things have a great influence on people around them as a result of their changed attitude to heaven and earth. A new spirit is drifting over our exhausted planet like a soft sea breeze. Perhaps this is the start of the clean-up operation of our seriously threatened environment. Admittedly the Revelation of St John reveals many prospective disasters, but this will be followed by great salvation. Are we actually observing the start of this now? Many people now believe that we have arrived in this apocalyptic age and for them the stories in this book serve as a confirmation of their suspicion. However, there will also be skeptical people who may say: "This apocalypse will not take place all that quickly and almost half of the stories you told could almost be explained in a "natural way". To them I would say: "What about the other half?"

They might counter this by saying that although there might not be any scientific explanation for those 50 stories, ten of them could for example be based on hypnosis. In that case we would still have another 40 stories. These people might say that ten of those 40 stories could possibly be explained by hallucinations. That still leaves 30.

They might become irritated and argue that ten of the 30 could have been made up. This still leaves 20 angels.

Finally they might say that another ten might be based on Jungian archetypes which have suddenly become active. (As though this is any real sort of explanation.)

Even then these skeptical people are still confronted with a number of inexplicable stories. They will encounter things which were impossible and which happened nevertheless.

If they were honest they would allow ten angels in their thoughts. Just imagine they did so . . . in that case the stories they have rejected would suddenly be viewed in a different light. For once you have pushed a button in yourself, you start to see the world from a new perspective. This gives you the chance to join in with the spiritual evolution which is taking place.

However, the sceptics will have problems. They grew up in a world in which scientific doubt has become elevated to a dogma so that there are no absolute truths. The ground has disappeared under their feet and they cannot breathe in this closed world. Therefore I would like to conclude with one last experience of an angel which is symbolic, as it were, of the whole book.

In this story you will clearly recognize the four stages of the experience:

– the personality before the experience (which I describe at the end of the story);
– the experience itself;
– the direct influence on that person;
– the long-term influence.

101 The woman this happened to is now 68 years old and was Polish by birth.

When she was 12 years old she went on a school trip with her fellow pupils. Somewhere in the Polish countryside, just outside Torun, they went swimming in an artificial pond, which was shallow at the side but deeper towards the centre. As she was playing with her friends she moved to a deeper part of the pond. She could not swim and went underwater. In an attempt to get her head above water she jumped up from the bottom but she soon noticed that she was being sucked down even deeper into the sandy bed. She stayed underwater and clearly felt that she would suffocate. Suddenly she saw her whole life passing in front of her in a flash and she realized that the end had come. She felt immensely saddened by the thought of her mother's great sorrow at losing her daughter. Then it happened! She felt a strong tug on her arm and was pulled up to the surface. When she thinks back to it now she can still feel that tug although all this happened 56 years ago. She floated slowly to the side of the pond. When she stood up the leader of the group said: "You must be a good swimmer if you went right to the middle of the pond." Then she added: "Child, you had such an angelic smile on your face, when you were lying on the water."

The girl did not say anything but walked into the woods by herself to thank God for the miracle by which had saved her life.

Although all the other girls were ill afterwards because they had swallowed some of the polluted water, she was not adversely affected in any way after being almost drowned.

Her experience changed her life to the extent that she was convinced that our existence in this world is not arbitrary. Moreover, this girl is a very clear example of my belief that experiences with angels do not happen to people by chance. She told me that when she was seven or eight years old she was occasionally overcome by a melancholy mood while her classmates were having fun, playing. She would sit quietly in a corner and ask herself why she had to live when she had to die in the end.

What was this Polish girl really feeling? Perhaps her soul was on the point of making the great change that is known as "rebirth". Perhaps she was like the bud of a waterlily. This is under pressure for a while before it bursts open in its full glory.

Why did I leave this story until last? The reason is that the experience of being pulled from the water is an ancient Biblical symbol. The meaning of the name Moses, the man who saved the people of Israel from Egypt, traditionally means "pulled from the water". This is a reference to the incident, just after his birth, when he was placed in a basket of reeds, on the banks of the Nile. According to another interpretation, the name Moses means: "he who pulls things from the water". This is a reference to his leadership during the journey through the Red Sea.

The word "tsaddic" translated in our Bible by "justice" is derived from the word for a "fish hook". A just person is therefore somebody who is drawn up from the water. We are submerged in our temporal life and can sink so far that we forget that we have been created for Eternity. Then He comes Who is involved in the miracle of catching fish (John 21) and He fishes us out of the water. Then we understand for ever that our lives on earth were a necessary training, preparing us for the new world we enter later and where all the tears will be wiped from our lives and we will be new creatures. However, we are not there yet. For the time being, we struggle on with our difficult existence.

Most of us do not see any angels at all, and hope that we make the best of it.

Let us not be discouraged if this does not always work. The hand which pulled the little girl out of the pond was not there for her alone. That hand is there for each of us, all our lives, and we only have to take hold of it to be pulled safely onto dry land.

The stories about angels in this book were not told to show the special things which happen to other people, but to tell everyone that we are watched over with love.

BIBLIOGRAPHY

Anoniem, *The Angels of Mons. A mystery from the First World War*, This England, 1982

Bakels, Floris, *Nacht und Nebel*, Elsevier, Amsterdam, 1978

Bin Gorion, Nicha Josef, *Die Sagen der Juden*, Insel Verlag, Frankfurt/M, 1962

Boom, Corrie ten, *Tramp for the Lord*, Fleming H. Revell Co., Old Tappan NJ, Verenigde Staten

Boon, Dr. R., *Over de goede engelen*, Boekencentrum, Den Haag

Bruin, Dr. Paul, *Bruder Klaus*, tijdschriftartikel, bron onbekend

Buck, Roland, *Angels on Assignment*, Hunter House Inc., Claremont CA, U.S.A.

Buck, Roland, *The Man Who Talked With Angels*, Son Life International

Buddingh, C., *Het gevleugelde hobbelpaard*, Het Spectrum, Utrecht, 1961

Bullinger, E. W. *How to enjoy the Bible*, The Lamp Press, 1955

Carlson Webber, Marilyn, *Angels, Angels, Everywhere*, in: Guideposts, Carmel NY, U.S.A.

Castaneda, Carlos, *Een aparte werkelijkheid*, De Bezige Bij, Amsterdam

Conradi, L. R., *De dienst der goede engelen*, International Traktaat Genoostschap, 1908

Crockett, Arthur, *Angels of the Lord*, Global Communications

Dante, *The Devine Comedy*, Penguin Books, London

Davidson, Gustav, *A Dictionary of Angels*, The Free Press, New York, 1967

Delarue, F. S., G. Buchwald, *Impfungen, der unglaubliche Irrtum*, Hirthammer, 1990

Dickens, Charles, *Een verhaal van Kerstmis*, Het Hollandse Uitgevershuis

Eersel, P. van, *La Source Noire*, Editions Grasset, Paris, 1986

Graaff, Dr. T. de, *Als goden sterven*, Lemniscaat, Rotterdam, 1970

Graham, Billy, *Angels, God's Secret Agents*, Hodder & Stoughton Christian Books, Sevenoaks, 1975

Grant, Myrna, *Vanya*, Gideon, Hoornaar, 1974

Halkin, Leon, *De biografie van Erasmus*, Tirion, Baarn

Hasselberch van Rijcken, Johan, *Verclaringhe heel wonderliker dinghen der werelt*, 1532

Heinen, *Heilende Erica*, Esotera Leserforum, Freiberg i/B

Hermann, Wolfgang, *Engel, gibt's die?* Lahn Verlag, Limburg

Hinz, Walther, *Woher – wohin?* ABC-Verlag, Zürich, 1980

Huber, George, *Gods engelen waken over ons*, Stadion

Hurt, Henry, *Een jongen, een slang en een engel*, in: Het Beste, October 1988, Readers Digest, Amsterdam

Acobs, J. J., *The monkey's paw and other stories*, Penguin Books, London

Jung, C. G., *De Catastrophe*, van Loghum, 1947

Knibb, M. A., *Het boek Henoch*, Ankh-Hermes, Deventer, 1983

Koch, K., *Seelsorge und Okkultismus*, Evangelisations Verlag

Kübler-Ross, E., *A letter to a child with cancer*, Shanti Nilaya

——, *Kinderen en de dood*, Ambo, Baarn

——, *Over de dood en het leven daarna*, Ambo, Baarn, 1985

Kuhlman, K., *Doet God nog wonderen?*, Gideon, Hoornaar

Lamborn Wilson, Peter, *Angels*, Thames and Hudson, London, 1980